The
FLINT CONEY

The FLINT CONEY

A SAVORY HISTORY

DAVE LISKE

AMERICAN PALATE

Published by American Palate
A Division of The History Press
Charleston, SC
www.historypress.com

Front cover, top: Flint Original Coney Island, and Nick's Coney Island. *Courtesy of the Sloan Museum Archives*; *bottom*: two Flint coneys at Gillie's in Mt. Morris, Michigan, on July 26, 2021. *Author's collection. Back cover, bottom*: George Brown Restaurant, which became Flint Original Coney Island in 1925. *Courtesy of the Sloan Museum Archives*.

First published 2022

Manufactured in the United States

ISBN 9781540251817

Library of Congress Control Number: 2021952415

Notice: The information in this book is true and complete to the best of our knowledge. It is offered without guarantee on the part of the author or The History Press. The author and The History Press disclaim all liability in connection with the use of this book.

This book is dedicated to my mother and father, Joyce and Erwin Liske, for ensuring the Flint coney was part of my life while growing up, and to my wife, Mary, and our kids, Caleb, Aaron, John, Adam, Briahna and Ryan, for eating their share of hundreds, if not thousands, of Flint coneys themselves during this obsession.

CONTENTS

ACKNOWLEDGEMENTS

INDIVIDUALS

Mary Yana (Todorovsky) Burau, longtime friend and member of the Atlas Coney Island family who answered numerous questions. She also loaned me her family's copy of *St. John St.: The "Melting Pot" Revisited*, 2nd ed. (Michael W. Evanoff, Edelweiss Press, 1984)

Monica Kass Rogers, owner at lostrecipesfound.com and a former food writer of the *Chicago Tribune*, for pointing me to the published recipe for "Gillie's Coney Island Chili Dogs."

Martha Parish, member of the Koegel Hotdogs Facebook group who, on January 31, 2015, posted a scan of food writer Joy Gallagher's *Flint Journal* column "Kitchen Clinic" of Tuesday, May 23, 1978, which included some of the folklore surrounding the ground hot dog coney sauce recipe, along with a possible Angelo's recipe using beef heart.

Jeanne Johnson Wright, member of the Koegel Hotdogs Facebook group who, on February 16, 2015, posted scans of the Ron Krueger columns from the 1990s that specifically refuted the claims of the recipes published by his predecessor, Joy Gallagher, particularly the folklore surrounding the sauce recipe containing ground hot dogs.

Vaughn Marlowe, a longtime Flint resident, who offered his remembrances of the Post Office Coney Island (which Marlowe recalled as the "Davison Road Coney Island"), owned by a John Nichols, the coney shop previously located at Davison Road at Franklin, where Angelo's operated until 2018. The Post Office Coney Island may have been the source of the Flint coney sauce recipe containing ground hot dogs.

CONEY ISLAND OPERATORS

Marty Embry, former owner, Tom Z's, Mt. Morris, and 51 to Go (Flint)

Dave Gillie, owner, Gillie's Coney Island, 6524 North Dort Highway (Mt. Morris)

Tom Zelevarovski, owner, Scotti's Coney Island (Burton), and former owner, Angelo's (Flint) and Tom Z's (Flint)

SUPPLIERS

Edward Abbott, president and CEO, Abbott's Meats (Flint)

John C. Koegel, president and CEO, Koegel Meats (Flint)

ARCHIVISTS

Johnathan Kirkwood, archivist, the Sloan Museum

INTRODUCTION

his work intends to correct people's perception of what the Flint coney really is and where it came from. We'll look at the historical context of Flint's early development as it related to food and what it was that brought together three men from three very different cultures and backgrounds—Simion Brayan from Boufi, Macedonia; Albert Koegel from Durlach, Germany; and Edward Abbott from Janesville, Wisconsin—to create the Flint coney. We'll see how the Balkan Wars of the early twentieth century caused so many Macedonian and Greeks to immigrate to the United States and how some of them ended up in Flint, along with how the automotive industry relates to some of the Flint coney's historic restaurant locations. The Greek and Macedonian Coney Island phenomenon itself will also be examined, including why so many of them established new roots in the United States within a period of just a few decades, how the need for a local gathering place was inspired by similar shops in their homelands and how the book-sized menus of Greek "classic" dishes developed beginning in the mid-twentieth century. The history of a popular "copycat" Flint coney sauce recipe containing ground beef, ground hot dogs and ketchup will be laid out, debunking the many dubious claims of its origin. Finally, we'll see where the Flint coney exists today and how that came to be.

One concept needs to remain clear: There is no such thing as a single restaurant recipe for Flint coney sauce. Since 1925, Abbott's Meat has provided a twenty-five-pound bag of sauce base, labeled "Coney Topping

A twenty-five-pound bag of uncooked and unseasoned Coney Topping Mix from Abbott's Meat, which has been provided to Flint Coney restaurants since 1925, with a ten-pound box of Koegel's Coney Franks. *Author collection.*

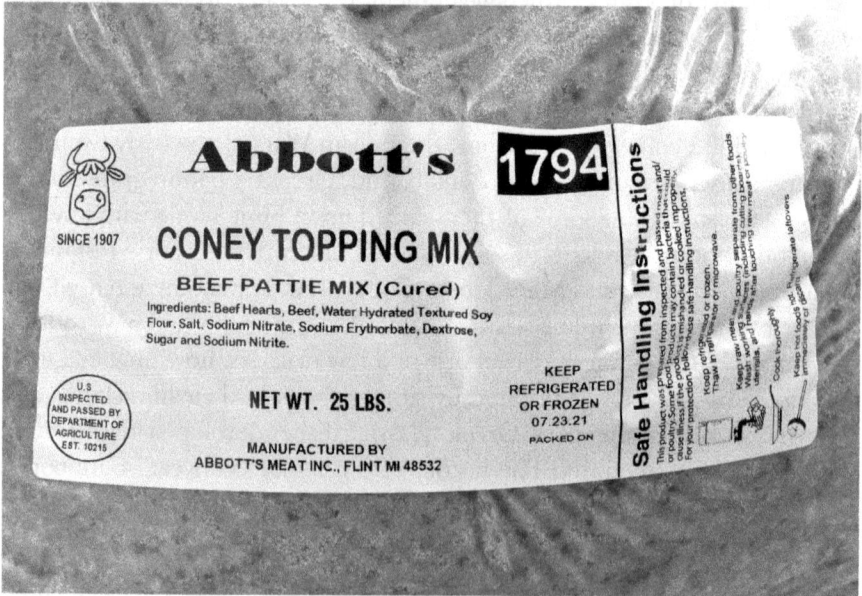

The label of the twenty-five-pound bag of Abbott's Coney Topping Mix. *Author collection.*

Mix: Beef Pattie Mix (Cured)" to restaurants. It currently consists of beef hearts, beef, water hydrated textured soy flour, salt, sodium nitrate, sodium erythorbate, dextrose, sugar and sodium nitrite. This raw and unfrozen product is the foundation for each restaurant's individual recipe for the sauce. How it's used by the cooks at each restaurant varies slightly, which is why there are so many minor variations in flavor and texture. That common sauce base from Abbott's is why all of the Flint coney sauces look the same and have similar textures. It's the individuality that creates the flavor and consistency differences.

While not an authorized biography of the described individuals and families whatsoever, I've labored in always remaining respectful to them and their respective cultures. If this is in any manner unclear, it's the fault of my own failure of language, unrelated to my honest feelings.

COMPANION WEBSITE

For updates to this book and further information, including a current list of restaurants serving the Flint coney, please visit my *Flint Coney Resource Site* at http://flintconeys.com.

MISSTEPS ALONG THE WAY

In researching the story of the Flint coney, I've definitely made mistakes in following what I had assumed was correct. Some of the work dates back more than a decade and should probably be looked at. This is particularly concerning as those works are still on the web with my name on them, and I am unable to access, modify or delete the earliest instance.

In October 2007, I attempted to branch out from the *Luna Pier Cook* blog I'd written for about a year, by writing a separate blog for MLive I had titled *Michigan Appetite*. MLive is a group of newspapers across the state of Michigan owned by a number of organizations over the years, currently Advance Publications/Booth Newspapers. The *Michigan Appetite* blog was to be in support of my broader efforts to identify and curate what I expected to call a "Michigan cuisine."

A post I wrote there on October 15, 2007, was titled "Recipe: 'Almost Flint-Style Coney Sauce', and Flint vs. Detroit Coneys."[1] This was my first attempt to write what I thought was an honest look at the Flint coney.

Unfortunately, I didn't even present that moniker correctly within the post. "At one time, coneys made with Angelo's coney sauce were called Flint-style coneys, although I'm not sure that's true any longer." That was a serious gaffe, but frankly I didn't know what I was saying at the time. The entire post also incorrectly presents Angelo's as the original Flint coney location, which I know now was wrong by twenty-four years, as well as being more than two miles from Simion Brayan's earlier Flint Coney Island at 202 South Saginaw Street.

Even worse was this paragragh:

> *If you head over to the Koegel Meats web site and search their Recipe page for the words "coney sauce" (minus the quotes) you'll currently find more than one version of this same recipe, each claiming to have been given to family members by someone who may or may not have been the person who developed Angelo's famous sauce.*

There are multiple problems with this paragraph:

1. The ground hot dog recipe in that post isn't how Flint coney sauce is made at restaurants.
2. Angelo's isn't where Flint coney sauce was developed.
3. Just because it's on the internet, even in a company-sponsored Facebook group, doesn't mean it's true.

It wasn't too long afterward that I began finding the facts I'd previously been unaware of. On January 28, 2009, I wrote a post on *Luna Pier Cook* titled "Michigan's Coney Sauces: Beef Heart? Kidneys?? The Realities Await...."[2] While there's still a bit of misinformation in that particular post (including a recipe I'd included for a Flint sauce that turned out to be inedible), it was at least a step in the right direction, far away from the MLive piece from two years earlier. On September 27, 2009, I then posted my first successful version of Flint coney sauce containing both beef heart and kidney as "Recipe: Authentic-Style Flint Coney Sauce."[3]

Mea culpa. Seriously.

1

BACKSTORIES

FOOD AND DINING IN EARLY FLINT

The settlement of Flint was quite small when the year 1831 rolled around, as "there were enough people for a Fourth of July Picnic behind [Jacob Smith's] house."[4] Throughout the nineteenth century, settlers and farmers planted wheat, corn and potatoes, along with breeding cattle, pigs, sheep and chickens. Game meats and fish were rather plentiful as well, and fur trading was one of the larger industries because there was so much game.[5] In their simple wood-fired hearths and cast-iron stoves, families prepared various breads and rolls, griddle cakes, egg dishes and rashers of bacon. Cucumbers were pickled, as were other vegetables, and fruit preserves were very common. Gingerbreads, fruit pies and several types of cakes were regular treats for a lot of families. These were served at the ends of meals of game, vegetable and potato soups and stews; roast or stewed venison, rabbit and wild turkey; and preparations of duck, fish and turtle. Chickens and geese were used in many types of dishes, as were all parts of the pig, sheep and cow. Tomatoes, onions and wild rice rounded out the flavors of the meals, as did handmade noodles and dumplings.[6]

Travelers who stayed in Flint would have had meals where they were staying, from the kitchens of the Northern Hotel, the Carleton House (renamed the Irving House and, after a fire in 1871, the site of the Bryant House) and the Lyon's Hotel. The Irving House alone saw as many as twenty-seven stagecoaches per day on the line from Holly to Saginaw, with

FLINT HIGH SCHOOL.

Flint High School, built in 1870. *From Ellis,* History of Genessee County, *1879.*

guests arriving specifically to have dinner there. The stagecoaches faded away as the passenger rail services began along the same routes in the 1860s. Locals and travelers alike would have also visited taverns such as John Todd's Flint River Tavern (aka the River House or simply Todd's Tavern) and Tom

Doyle's saloon.[7] A "tavern" of the day wasn't what we're familiar with today. It was more akin to a one-room cabin, open to travelers needing a place to stay. "Dinner" may have been a simple meal of salt pork, cornbread, cooked greens and potatoes, with water or whiskey as beverages. Blankets hung on thin rope or string strung across the room would have divided single-room taverns for the night, with men on the floor and women possibly in the host's bed. Later taverns had real dining rooms with bars, with either the one large room or individual guest rooms being on the second floor.[8]

At Todd's Tavern,

> *The landlord was able to gratify the taste of the most fastidious epicure in the variety of his menu, game of all kinds being abundant. The vegetables for the table were easily cultivated, while venison, wild turkeys, and fish, as well as maple-sugar, were supplied by the Indians, with "fire-water" being regarded as a legal tender in payment for all their wares. A pint of whisky (and this, as a matter of precaution, diluted) would purchase a saddle of venison, and a turkey weighing twenty-five pounds could be had for double the quantity.…Upon the establishment of the land-office at the Grand Traverse, "Todd's Tavern" became so popular a rendezvous that its capacity was unequal to the demands upon it. Crowds of land-seekers pressed their claims for food and shelter, and many were content to wait for hours their turn at the often-replenished table.*[9]

Flint grew as various industries expanded. Horse-drawn carriages were built in Flint as early as 1839. The population was a mere two thousand when the city was incorporated in 1855. Most of the roads were still dirt, and according to lumberman Henry Crapo, split shingles were a form of local currency instead of the less stable state currency. A future governor of the state of Michigan, Crapo initially moved to Flint from Massachusetts in 1855. By 1858, Crapo's company was sawing seven million board feet of lumber in two mills. Flint became a popular lumbering hub, and by 1870 the population had grown to five thousand. The downtown area saw steam locomotives pulling both freight and passenger trains through it on a regular basis. The Flint & Pere Marquette Railway was completed on December 8, 1862, operating between Flint and Saginaw. Crapo also opened his lumber freight and passenger service, the Flint & Holly Railroad, only two years later on November 1, 1864, with coordinated passenger service between those two cities and the Detroit & Milwaukee Railroad beginning in early 1865. The Grand Trunk Railway running passenger and freight east–west through Flint was developed in the late 1870s. The Flint & Pere Marquette line was purchased by Crapo in 1900 and became known simply as the Pere Marquette Railway.[10]

Toward the end of the 1800s, Flint was just like any other town at the time. When the climate was dry and warm, dust from the unpaved roads would fill the air in a haze. The smell of both the burning wood fire under the boilers and the steam from the locomotives permeated everything nearby. Chimneys throughout Flint exhausted smoke and steam from the hearths, stoves and ovens of homes, hotels and restaurants where local meats, game, breads, vegetables and fruit were used in dishes from the various European cultures and ethnic groups that made up the city. All those wonderful smells came together to add an air of heartiness to the already hardworking residents. The city was ready to grow in a way no resident then could have possibly imagined.

THE HOT DOG

The history of the hot dog dates to the thirteenth century, when pork sausages became popular in Frankfurt, Germany. One of the more incorrect claims about the hot dog is that the handheld food is an American invention. In examining the history of the hot dog, the National Hot Dog and Sausage Council has indicated that the frankfurter was apparently known as a "dachshund" or "little dog" sausage as offered by Johann Georghehner in Coburg, Germany, in the late 1600s.[11] The city of Vienna then saw a pork and beef blend of the frankfurter in about the eighteenth century, when it started being referred to as a wiener.[12] The history then becomes quite murky, with competing claims of the first instance of what would become the hot dog. This work won't go into all of those stories here, as there are far too many of them.

The one development that would be important to the Coney Island hot dog is that a gentleman named Thomas Feltman emigrated from Germany in 1856 at the age of fifteen. In 1867, he was selling meat pies from a wagon on Coney Island when he came up with what he called the "red hot." He then opened Feltman's German Gardens, also on Coney Island, in about 1870. Feltman subsequently turned this into a lucrative resort, with rides and restaurants, and by 1920 was serving an estimated five million customers each year.[13]

Feltman's on Coney Island, sometime between 1930 and 1945, a postcard published by Tichnor Bros., Inc., Boston. *Courtesy of the Boston Public Library.*

In 1913, the Coney Island Chamber of Commerce in New York banned the use of the term *hot dog* on restaurant signs on Coney Island.[14] This action was prompted by visitors taking the term too literally, assuming there was dog meat in the sausage itself. Because of this action by the chamber of commerce, immigrants passing through the area didn't know the sausage in a bun by the American moniker *hot dog*. Instead, the handheld food was known to immigrants as a "Coney Island."[15]

It then becomes clear that the hot dog as the sausage itself is a German development, regardless of American claims to the contrary. Both the German frankfurter, and the action by the Coney Island Chamber of Commerce, would end up being integral aspects of the story of the Flint coney.

IS THE HOT DOG A SANDWICH?

Personally, I don't believe the hot dog is a sandwich. Consider this: When someone goes to the store for a "pack of hot dogs," the buns aren't included in the package of frankfurters or similar sausages of German origin. People might shop for a particular type or brand of hot dog, but the buns are more likely in another part of the store altogether. Hot dogs are never manufactured and cured or smoked in the same facility the bun is baked in. The claim that the hot dog is only named so because of the added bun is therefore false, even though they're most often served one within the other in North America.

There are also many who claim that a hot dog in any form is a sandwich and that, by extension, a coney dog is a sandwich as well. This claim runs against definitions in the *Oxford English Dictionary*.

A sandwich is defined by the *Oxford English Dictionary* as "an item of food consisting of two pieces of bread with a filling between them, eaten as a light meal." This is different from its definition of a hot dog as "a frankfurter, especially one served hot in a long, soft roll and topped with various condiments." Even more telling is the Oxford definition for a frankfurter, which is "a small, cooked and smoked sausage of beef or beef and pork." These latter definitions clearly describe a hot dog as a "frankfurter," in other words, as the meat itself, without any type of bread product.[16]

Therefore, a hot dog on its own is not a sandwich in any form.

A Coney Island hot dog is then a hot dog, in a long, soft roll, with toppings. *Oxford* defines a coney dog as "a type of hot dog topped with chili con carne (without beans), raw onion, and mustard." It's the "long, soft roll" that makes the difference. *Oxford* also makes this differentiation in its definition of a submarine sandwich: "a sandwich made of a long roll filled with meat, cheese, and vegetables such as lettuce, tomato, and onions." Here the item is called a sandwich in the definition, which does not occur in the definitions of either a hot dog or a coney dog.[17]

Clearly, as there are not two slices of bread involved in the *Oxford* definition, the dictionary states that a coney dog is not a sandwich, as opposed to other definitions within the work which explicitly state that a defined item is a sandwich.

ORIGINATORS OF THE FLINT CONEY

Like many seemingly ubiquitous products and food items of today, the development of the Flint coney involved one man's vision and the rich skills of a couple of experts in their fields. In the case of the Flint coney, the two experts were Irishman Edward Abbott and German immigrant Albert Koegel.

Edward Patrick Abbott was born on September 24, 1872, in Janesville, Wisconsin. Both of his parents were Irish, and by age sixteen or seventeen

Edward was working as a butcher at the Nels Carlson Meat Market at 29 North Main Street in Janesville in 1889.[18]

A few thousand miles to the east, Albert Koegel was born on October 18, 1884, in Germany and raised in the city of Durlach.[19] When he was of age, he joined one of Germany's well-respected apprenticeship programs under the supervision of a master butcher. In a few years, he had earned his Meister Wurstmacher designation, indicating he was a master sausage maker.[20]

For anyone craving Flint coneys or who's spent time looking for an "authentic" sauce recipe, the village to go back to was at one time known as Boufi, in the prefecture of Florina in the pre-1913 Macedonian region of Greece. It was a relatively small village of only a couple thousand people who, after the dawn of the twentieth century, would find themselves in a conflict that the rest of the world would find absolutely appalling. That conflict would drive most of them out of that region, causing them to flee thousands of miles across the Atlantic, some of them ending up in Flint, Michigan, with one of them ultimately creating an endearing cultural phenomenon that would have an appeal that has lasted for multiple generations.

The man with the vision was Simion Petcieff Brayan. The main player in the story of the Flint coney, Brayan was born on September 9, 1889,

Simion Brayan's World War II draft registration card. *Selective Service Records, National Archives at St. Louis, via ancestry.com.*

in the village of Boufi, which he listed as "Buffe" on his World War II draft registration card much later at the age of fifty-one. (That village is also named as "Buff" or "Bouf" in other references.)[21] But there are a couple of other details that can be a bit confusing. His father is listed in some records as Petio but apparently was a Branoff, not a Brayan. Simion's mother may have been named Petra, but there's no clear record of this. And Simion listed a George Branoff, not "Brayan," as a cousin on the line for "Name and address for person who will always know your address" on that draft registration card.

Members of the Brayan/Branoff family have always understood the names Branoff and Brayan are the same name. The family has also understood Simion changed his name from Brayanis to Brayan when he came to America, as did others. Meanwhile, some of the Branoffs chose the name Brown, while others maintained the Branoff name, which confuses the family history even further. The Branoff and Brown names among the Flint-area Macedonians, all likely Brayan's cousins, are scattered throughout the history of the Flint coney, most of those family members having emigrated from Boufi.[22]

One particular spelling of the name of the village, Boufi, is the one that also shows up in news reports and official documentation from the time, which is why I'm using that spelling in this work.[23]

Some question the validity of stating that Macedonia was a country until its declared independence on September 8, 1991, or its recognition by the United Nations on April 8, 1993. Macedonians have always believed that country to be theirs. It doesn't matter how many of them feel that way or how many people disagree with them. It's the feelings of the Macedonians that matter.

Macedonians reflect a certain ethnicity. They have considered themselves separate from invaders and those who would annex them for more than a century before the UN recognition. Immigration records from the early 1900s show their passion for claiming to be Macedonian, not Greek, Bulgarian or any other.[24] The proud people of Macedonia considered their country to be its own place with its own considerations, regardless of what other country may have claimed otherwise over many decades or centuries.[25] It's out of respect for those individuals and their inherent ethnicity that we need to keep their history, their culture, their own sense of country alive, and not suppress it with the opinions of others.

FOOD AND DINING IN OLD MACEDONIA

Michael W. Evanoff was a Flint lawyer who became the autoworkers' first lawyer after the sit-down strike of 1937, as well as a Flint author and historian. He wrote a four-hundred-page volume on the history of the "melting pot" of cultures in the St. John Street area of Flint that honors each ethnic group in its own regard. In her own chapter, his mother, Lenka, described a number of Macedonian foods and dishes. She began with "turshea," generally peppers or cucumbers preserved in vinegar, a "Macedonian salad" of mixed greens with oil and vinegar identified with that term in France and Tetovo beans, which are difficult to find elsewhere. There were also pastries such as gevrek, lokum (aka "Turkish Delight") and "baklavah" of different regional varieties. Lenka went into great detail in numerous places in her chapter in describing Turkish coffee, a staple at most meals, meetings and personal meet-ups. There was also "tava yogurt" made by Turks, which could be cut with a knife, as well as regional fruits and olives, and an incredible number of breads including pastermailije ("a flat bread with a quantity of pork pieces"), bakardan (similar to pastermailije but made with cornmeal), simit ("a small flat loaf of bread with seeds in it") and mafishe ("flattened pastry dough in a square and the ends gathered in the center, then covered with honey or sweetened liquid").

While corn is generally thought of as an American item, Lenka Evanoff described how important it was in Macedonian culture. Both sweet and other corns were grown in Macedonia. She detailed a few dishes made with corn, including the making of a sweet-and-sour drink called "boza." She also described the rituals surrounding the butchering of hogs and the resulting preparations of knuckles and feet, and the sausages that would be made from the meat.

A stew Lenka described seems of importance to our story:

> As for "chumlek," here again one starts with cuts of beef and into the pot is poured some wine or vinegar, a cup of water, red and black pepper, salt and cloves. The pot is covered and placed in the oven for cooking. Here again one tests the meat for doneness and at the right time there is added onions and a considerable amount of garlic. The components need to be put in and cooked at the right time and to the right degree in order for the whole to be of the right consistency and taste. With chumlek, the dish is so good that one enjoys it without any problem with the garlic.[26]

CULTURAL BEGINNINGS AND THE BALKAN WARS

The village of Boufi, Florina, Macedonia, was quite small, but numerous violent events happened there. As of the late twentieth century, the renamed village of Akritas had a population of only around two hundred, depending on the source of the record, down from about two thousand a century earlier. The events that occurred there in the early 1900s were downright brutal and require a closer look, as they were the cause of a mass emigration from the area to other parts of the world.

In the early twentieth century, the prefecture of Florina was in turmoil, along with the rest of Macedonia. On August 23, 1903, the *Los Angeles Herald* reported that the previous day, "the villages of Boufi, Rakaro and Armcsko, near Florina, have been bombarded and their insurgent garrisons annihilated. At Boufi alone 500 Bulgarians are reported to have been killed. The women and children escaped to the mountains."[27] In 1914, the *Report of the International Commission to Inquire into the Causes and Conduct of the Balkan Wars*, from the Carnegie Endowment for International Peace, stated that during this time "there are a thousand deaths and, in the final result, 200 villages ruined by Turkish vengeance, 12,000 houses burned, 3,000 women outraged, 4,700 inhabitants slain and 71,000 without a roof."[28]

In Macedonia, during another Balkan War in the summer of 1913, it seems Boufi remained untouched, as there is apparently nothing described in official documentation. The fighting appears to have happened elsewhere, most of the atrocities occurring east of Florina in villages such as Serres and Doxato. But as it had been only ten years since the 1903 atrocities in Boufi and residents had fled, it's quite possible there was simply not much left. Boufi was later renamed Akritas as per the Treaty of Bucharest in 1913, when the Florina prefecture was granted to Greece.[29]

Michael Evanoff described later visiting Boufi and the issues he and his wife, Genevieve, found:

> *Those who came from the old country were from the area of Lerin and Buff, Greek Macedonia. For the most part their employment in the Flint area was in the coney island business, starting with the Flint Original Coney Island....We made many attempts but were never able to locate [Buff] because the name had been changed to Agritas [sic]....We were stopped by the military and taken to their command post for interrogation....They served us Turkish coffee and found an elderly man [who] could speak a little English. We were able to explain our presence in the area....They*

Къмъ № № 61—67. — Бѣжанци отъ с. Горно Броди (Сѣреко), настанени въ гр. Пещера. Между тѣхъ има много вдовици и сирачета на мжже убити и изчезнали.

TERRITORIAL MODIFICATIONS
IN THE BALKANS
1. CONFERENCE OF LONDON   2. TREATY OF BUKAREST

Boufi / Akritas
approximate location
(maps are not to scale)

Above: Bulgarian refugee children from Ano Vrontou (Gorno Brodi), Greece, after they lost their parents in the Second Balkan War. These children were resettled by international aid agencies in the city of Pestera, Bulgaria. *Photo by Verlag Ernst Siegfried Mittler und Sohn, 1913, public domain.*

Left: Maps showing the shifts of the boundaries of various territories resulting from the London Peace Conference of 1912–13 (*top*) and the 1913 Treaty of Bucharest (*bottom*). *Carnegie Endowment for International Peace 1914; Boufi location by the author.*

invited us to come back the following day…and they would help us find Buff. The village is close to Lerin or Florina, where some of the immigrants from Buff in the Flint area have relatives living and operating businesses. The village of Buff itself has shrunk to a very low number as a result of all of the emigration.…I believe one might safely that most of the coney islands in the Flint area are owned and operated by Macedonians from the Lerin-Buff-Bitola, and Presspa regions of Yugoslav Macedonia.[30]

Google Street View imaging of the main road through Akritas was completed in August 2011. Viewers can see the state of the village at that time, including numerous abandoned homes and businesses, as well as construction equipment in front of the two-story Primary School of Akrita, which was originally completed in 1910.

Meanwhile in Wisconsin, Edward Abbott married Frances Josephine McMahon on June 7, 1904, and apparently relocated to Waukesha.[31] Records don't indicate why he ultimately moved to Flint, but there are two distinct possibilities. Suppliers and other people passing through Wisconsin were already talking about the manufacturing opportunities in Michigan, along with the need for other industries and services in those manufacturing areas. Some folks were relocating because of this information alone.[32] But another possibility is that it was a business move. Cudahy Packing was opened by Patrick and John Cudahy southeast of Milwaukee in 1872 in what is now Cudahy, Wisconsin, which was named after the company.[33] When the Abbott family moved to Flint, Edward became the manager of the Cudahy Meat Outlet, named the "Peoples Cash Meat Outlet," at 124 East Kearsley Street.[34] It's possible Abbott's move to Flint was at the request of the Cudahy brothers.

Regardless of why the move occurred, Edward and Frances showed up on the Genesee County census of 1910.[35] The Cudahy Meat Outlet in Flint, aka the People's Cash Meat Market, had apparently opened in 1907.[36] According to his World War I draft registration card, the shop was still owned by the Cudahys when Edward signed that card on September 4, 1918.[37] Cudahy still operated ninety-five of its own meat outlets in 1922, so the change to Abbott's Meat may have been after that date. The date of the name change is unclear, as Abbott's still uses 1907 as its founding year in marketing.

Across the Atlantic in Germany in 1911, Albert Koegel paid one hundred dollars for passage and boarded the steamship SS *Main* in Bremen, an enclosed passenger vessel configured to transport 369 first-class, 217 second-class and 2,865 third-class passengers. (The *Main*'s manifest had him listed

Edward Patrick Abbott's draft registration card, completed on September 4, 1918. Under "Employer's Name," he wrote "Cudahy Bros." *From Martyn, Martyn Family History online.*

as "Albert Keegel.") Twenty-six-year-old Albert arrived in New York on November 9, 1911. The manifest had his destination listed as Milwaukee, Wisconsin,[38] where he found work as the supervisor of Twin City Packing, a butchering plant that had opened in the 1890s in the twin border lumbering communities of Marinette, Wisconsin, and Menominee, Michigan.[39]

HEADING TO FLINT

In his book *Michigan in Four Centuries*, Dr. F. Clever Bald, a history professor at the University of Michigan and assistant director of the university's Michigan Historical Collection, wrote,

> *The period 1890 to 1920 was marked by many social, political and economic changes* [in Michigan].... *The increase in manufacturing caused a shifting of population from the rural districts to the cities. Detroit, Grand Rapids, Flint and Pontiac grew rapidly....During this period*

*immigration to the United States was unrestricted in spite of protests
by workingmen. Foreigners continued to come to Michigan, but new
nationalities predominated. While the number of Scandinavian immigrants
was sufficient only to maintain the level previously reached, there was a
marked increase in the number of Poles, Hungarians, Greeks, and Italians.
Fewer Scots, Irish, and English came to Michigan.*[40]

Family history indicates Albert Koegel collected used meatpacking
equipment from the lumberjacks and hoped to acquire a plant to the west
in North Dakota.[41] Multiple reports also indicate that "a salesman from the
Armour Company told him it was a crazy idea [to open a plant in North
Dakota]. 'There is nothing out there. You should go to Flint, Michigan—it's
the hottest city in the country right now because of the auto industry.'" This
follows what other immigrants were being told about the area. Albert made
the move to Flint and established the first location of Koegel's Meats in 1916
as a retail meat market at 116 West Kearsley Street.[42]

In Boufi, Simion married Velicia Vishen in 1909, and Velicia gave birth to
Anastasia, aka Anna, in 1912.[43] But by then, people were leaving the area in
droves as the Balkan Wars continued. Macedonian and Greek immigration
to the United States subsequently increased in rather significant numbers.
The Carnegie report lists Greek immigration to the United States on page
391, beginning with 172 immigrants in the year 1885 (the number of
steamers being 78) and climbing with a rapid steadiness to 36,580 in 1907
before leveling off, the chart finishing with a number of 37,021 in 1911 (the
number of steamers being 347). The total number from 1900 to 1911 alone
was 208,237 Greek refugees, which were part of a much larger number of
unrelated emigrations from all countries combined.[44]

Brayan immigrated to the United States on October 6, 1916, aboard the
SS *Re d'Italia* from Napoli, with his final destination listed as the home of a
cousin, Tim Brayan, in Youngstown, Ohio.[45] It must be noted that Simion
immigrated alone. Velicia (née Vishen) and Anna (Anastasia) didn't make
the same trip until 1925, arriving at Ellis Island aboard the *Olympic* on April
30. Brayan's wife's first name was listed on the manifest as "Velica"; their
last name was recorded as "Brayanni," and Boufi was listed, once again
incorrectly, as "Bouto."[46] Sons Peter, Boris and Carl were born later in Flint.

Why was there such a large gap between Simion Brayan's immigration
and that of his wife and child? As we'll see shortly, he didn't head directly for
Flint. But there were other issues as well. As Lenka Evanoff described in her
son Michael's cultural history volume, those kinds of delays were normal, if,

in fact, the rest of the family immigrated at all. She told the story of meeting her husband, Kosta, in an arrangement at the age of fourteen, marrying a year later and having to become a single mother in Macedonia with two-year-old Miso (Michael) and his year-old brother, Fore (Frank), when Kosta left for America in 1913 to avoid military service with the Turkish army to oppress his own people. He arrived at Ellis Island on December 7, 1913, aboard the *Caronia* from Liverpool, England. However, Lenka was unaware of Kosta's safe arrival for four years.[47]

People left the Balkan region for various reasons, including avoiding religious persecution or to look for better family income. Tragically, as Lenka wrote,

> *There were many examples, however, when men never returned and in many cases, never made arrangements to have their family come to them. They just forgot their family for all practical purposes and made a new life even taking on new wives in America or in some of the other countries, without taking the trouble to put an end to the old marriage. Divorces were practically non-existent in the Balkans and wives left behind forever lived in blackness, neither single or really married.*[48]

Fortunately for Lenka Evanoff, and Velicia Brayan and their children, this didn't happen to them. Lenka and her children suffered through numerous Balkan wars and battles from all sides, as well as World War I. They were then able to emigrate from Macedonia in 1921 via horse and carriage, on trains to Switzerland and France, to a ship called the *Paris* at Le Havre, arriving at Ellis Island, then to a home run by the Hebrew Immigrant Aid Society in New York City and finally to where Kosta was living in Cleveland, ultimately moving to Flint in 1925.[49]

2

ORIGINS OF THE FLINT CONEY

A "CONEY" IN ROCHESTER, NEW YORK

The etymology of the term "Coney Island hot dog" or "coney dog" turns out to be confusing at best. Legend states that immigrants would leave Ellis Island and, passing through the Coney Island resort area, then eat at Feltman's or Nathan's Famous. They would then establish their own restaurant at their destination, serving their own version of what they called a "Coney Island hot dog." An example of this would be Thomas and Kalliopi Nickolson, who went through Coney Island in 1920 and founded Red Hots Coney Island in Highland Park, Michigan, in 1921.[50]

Simion Brayan's own story takes a different path from the Nickolsons but still ends up with the same result. But Brayan's physical path after his 1916 immigration took a completely unexpected turn.

It turns out there is a second immigration record for Brayan, at the port city of Buffalo, New York. According to the St. Albans Lists, he immigrated to that city from Canada on May 9, 1921, reporting that the last time he immigrated to the United States was on October 7, 1916, aboard the SS *Re d'Italia*, while also listing Velicia as his wife.[51] Apparently, Brayan traveled from Ellis Island on October 6 and headed for Youngstown, Ohio, as per the 1916 document. It's unclear exactly where his travels took him from there, as the May 1921 U.S. immigration record from Buffalo listed his last place of permanent residence as Toronto, Canada, and his occupation as "fur dryer."

Details of Simion Brayan's three-page immigration record at Buffalo, New York, on May 9, 1921. *National Archives and Records Administration, 1921.*

There's no public record of exactly when Brayan went to Toronto or why. The government of Canada explains why this record cannot yet be found:

> *From 1908 to 1918, and from 1925 to 1935, border entry records were compiled in a list format to record the names of immigrants....From January 1, 1919 to December 31, 1924, the Department of Immigration and Colonization required that individual forms (Form 30) be completed and submitted to the immigration officers at border ports, instead of the large sheet border-entry lists previously in use....Please note that the border*

entry records are only about 50% complete. Not all immigrants crossed the border at official ports, or, if the port was closed at the time, they would have entered the country without being registered.[52]

Brayan's destination as reported for the 1921 immigration record was a friend's house, a Mr. Kosher [*sic*] at 54 Court Street in Buffalo.[53]

It's been reported that Brayan visited a lunch counter in Rochester, New York. This was likely while he was in Buffalo after his second immigration in 1921. He reportedly ordered what they called a "Coney Island," then quoted as saying it was "practically tasteless...unfit for a young man whose palate was accustomed to the hardy cuisine of southeast Europe....They used ground beef, a little chili powder, a little paprika, but it had no taste." Thinking back to the Macedonian goulash he'd eaten back in Boufi, which contained beef heart and occasionally beef kidney, all in a beef suet base, he determined he could make a better coney sauce based on the heartiness of that Macedonian dish.[54]

In the preceding paragraph I wrote that he "supposedly ordered what they called a 'Coney Island.'" I phrased it that way because the shop likely wouldn't have offered a "Coney Island hot dog" as we know it today. The Rochester area was well known for Feltman's red hot, which is a frankfurter, and is even more well known for a more local Weisswurst-like sausage offering known as a "white hot". The white hot was originally made from lesser-quality and less expensive meats and fillers than the red hot, although they're now made with higher-quality ingredients. Restaurants in the Rochester area serve both the red hot and the white hot, which are both occasionally topped with a dry sauce that's remarkably similar in consistency to the later Flint coney sauce.

What's most important to note about the white hot is that, on some menus in Rochester and the Syracuse areas, it is sometimes referred to as a "coney." But on others, it is not. For example, Heid's of Liverpool outside Syracuse, established in 1917, currently lists the white hot as a "coney" on its menu.[55] Also, the Hofmann Sausage Company in Syracuse has produced a "coney" white hot since 1932, recently renaming the product on the label as the "Snappy Griller."[56] The sausage is not referred to as a "Coney Island," but the implied genealogy of the name from Coney Island in New York City is there because of Feltman's red hot being listed on those same restaurant menus in the area.

It's difficult to determine exactly when Brayan arrived in Flint. He doesn't show up in city directories until 1926,[57] although we know from the timeline

A retail package of Hofmann Snappy Grillers, offered on restaurant menus as coneys in Upstate New York. *Author collection.*

of events surrounding the Flint coney (which is outlined later) he arrived earlier than that. According to census records, Paul Brown immigrated in 1922, with Paul's own wife, Velicia, immigrating on November 9, 1929. Paul's wife's last name, however, was listed on the manifest for the ship *Berengaria* as "Branoff."[58]

The address Simion Brayan's wife, Velicia, gave as her destination when she immigrated in 1925 was 20240 Saginaw Street.[59] (That address doesn't exist; "2240" makes much more sense. Most people would say 2240 as "twenty-two forty," which could certainly be misinterpreted as "20240.") The 1930 Flint census, however, indicates the family was living at 410 Lyon Street, which Simion Brayan likely built in the late 1920s after his wife, Velicia, and daughter Anna had immigrated. The same census also shows Paul and Velicia Branoff were living with the Brayans at the time.[60]

THE CREATION OF THE FLINT CONEY SAUCE

The creative moment for the Flint coney is when Simion Brayan decided to develop and sell a better hot dog sauce than what he'd eaten at that lunch counter in Rochester, New York. From the information we have so far, and the fact that Brayan didn't settle in the United States until after 1921, it becomes clear that the development of the Flint coney likely occurred in Flint sometime between 1922 and 1925.

There has been considerable public confusion about the existence of a single recipe for Flint coney sauce. There was a single recipe at one time, when Brayan's Flint Coney Island was the only shop in town from 1925 (the shop first appeared in city directories in 1926)[61] to his first competitors opening a few years later. Since that time, there have been dozens of recipes, literally a recipe for each Flint coney restaurant. How that happened is part of the overall story.

What seems to have been lost in public perception of the history of the Flint coney is that Abbott's Meat didn't make a complete sauce for Brayan's or any other restaurant until just before the turn of the twenty-first century. (The completed retail version Abbott's offers today in four- and ten-pound bags is a recent development.) In speaking with me about his own history at Starlite Coney Island beginning in 1973, in early 2015 David Gillie of Gillie's Coney Island told me, "They used the twenty-five-pound raw extra-fine grind of 'beef heart, beef and soy texture' from Abbott's Meat." Abbott's provided the raw, unfrozen and unspiced sauce base to the restaurants, nothing more.

Making Flint coney sauce is relatively simple. Edward Abbott has specifically stated, "The only meat ingredient is beef heart regardless of the stories and rumors of other meat parts being used."[62] Beef suet is melted, and finely chopped onions are sautéed in the hot fat. When the onions are translucent, the restaurant's own combination of spices is added. Those spices include good amounts of cumin and chili powder (generally about eight ounces each), maybe some savory Spanish or smoked paprika (not Hungarian, which is either sweet or hot paprika) and whatever else they'd like. Once the spices are blended into the onion and fat mixture, the twenty-five pounds of raw extra fine grind of "beef, beef heart and soy texture" from Abbott's Meat is added, along with any other ground meat components the restaurant might use, such as beef kidney or liver. The sauce is then allowed to simmer for more than an hour to tenderize the ground beef heart to the right consistency.

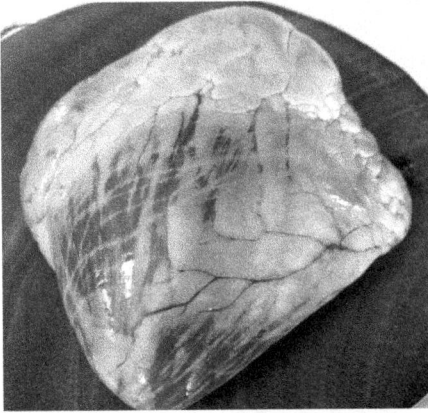

Left: A whole beef heart, approximately 4.25 pounds, the main ingredient in Flint Coney sauce. *Author collection.*

Below: A retail jar of beef tallow, with the described bulk spices as found at Gordon Food Service (GFS). Opening the jar of tallow gives an immediate smell similar to that of cooked beef brisket. As many restaurants in the Flint area receive truck shipments from GFS, these particular spice bottles are common. *Author collection.*

Edward Abbott stated, "[We] added some seasoning, but each owner added spices of his own, not so much to preserve a 'secret recipe' as to maintain quality."[63]

One-time coney operator Marty Embry once told me, "The thing about coney sauce is that it is interpretive. There are many ways to make a form of coney sauce, and from that point it becomes a preference. You tend to prepare it based on preference of flavors and palate." Many of the early coney operators began their working lives at Brayan's Flint Coney Island, taking the recipe and their own modifications with them to start their own Coney Islands while passing on that knowledge to future operators as well.

This traceable "pedigree" explains why every Flint coney restaurant has its own distinct variation and its own followers who are accustomed to that specific flavor and texture, while still maintaining the Flint coney "style."

And for the record, no known restaurant Flint coney sauce recipe has ever included ground hot dogs, contrary to popular folklore. Details of where that folklore came from can be found in chapter 5.

Once he was settled in Flint after 1921, Simion Brayan spoke with an Abbott's Meat employee about his concept of using Macedonian goulash containing beef heart and kidney as the basis for his Flint coney sauce.[64] It's likely that his own recipe for Flint coney sauce was never written down. At the time of the development of the sauce, home cooks generally didn't write down their recipes. Any documentation of Brayan's original recipe itself may not have ever existed.

DECLINING PUBLIC ACCEPTANCE OF BEEF HEART

A large part of the population of the United States today exhibits a squeamishness about many types of foods the rest of the world eats, including the offal that's an integral part of the sauce for the Flint coney.[65] It's quite possible this could be part of the reason many people are more accepting of Flint coney sauce recipes that don't use beef heart or kidney: many today can't seem to handle the thought of eating such things.

Making the above statement is a matter of personal experience. One of my rules for my own kids has always been, "You can't say you don't like a food unless you actually try it first." Because of this, our kids as adults are still quite the "adventurous eaters." Our kids will try, and likely enjoy, just about anything, from blood-tongue sausage, to head cheese, eel, octopus, crawfish, tripe in the Mexican soup called menudo, beef tongue in lengua tacos—and yes, beef heart. My wife also enjoys sliced and fried beef testicles in the dish that's politely called "Rocky Mountain Oysters," a popular item on (ironically enough) appetizer menus at restaurants in Cody, Wyoming.

However, an issue did develop with the beef hearts in authentic Flint coney sauce. My wife and our daughter became squeamish about eating the coney only after they learned the heart was the main ingredient. Nothing changed: The recipe certainly didn't change, as the amount of heart on each coney is nearly identical regardless of the restaurant. Only their perception of the enjoyability of the dish changed.

Sliced and fried bull testicles, aka Rocky Mountain Oysters, at the Irma Hotel in Cody, Wyoming, on February 28, 2021. *Author collection.*

I put *adventurous eaters* in quotations earlier, as it's an American misnomer: being an adventurous eater means only that you're willing to try foods other peoples and cultures eat each and every day. Ironically though, the term also belies the fact that the U.S. population hasn't always been this way. Adventurous eaters in the United States are, in fact, quite a recent development.

While the phrase "nose-to-tail eating" may appear to be a recent fad, it is how the rest of the world eats. At the same time, because the United States is a nation of immigrants, such meals used to be standard fare in American households and restaurants. "Nose-to-tail eating" is actually a return to those earlier dishes, not anything new. This can be seen in recipes in earlier editions of popular American cookbooks, with many of those recipes no longer appearing in current versions of the same cookbooks. For example, the current publication known as *The Fanny Farmer Cookbook* was first published as *The Boston Cooking School Cook Book* in 1896. Fannie Merritt Farmer was principal of the school at the time, having taken over the position from Mary J. Lincoln in 1891. Farmer died on January 16, 1915, but the 1921 edition of the cookbook as well as later editions still bore her name as author. The 1915 and 1921 editions contained recipes for calf's liver, sweetbreads, tripe, calf's heads and tongues and braised ox joints. Two recipes for stuffed beef heart were also included:

Calf's Heart
Wash a calf's heart, remove veins, arteries, and clotted blood. Stuff (using half quantity of Fish Stuffing I on page 164, seasoned highly with sage) and sew. Sprinkle with salt and pepper, roll in flour, and brown in hot fat. Place in small, deep baking pan, half cover it with boiling water, cover closely, and bake slowly two hours, basting every fifteen minutes. It may be necessary to add more water. Remove heart from pan, and thicken the liquor with flour diluted with a small quantity of cold water. Season with salt and pepper, and pour around the heart before serving.

***

Fish Stuffing I
¼ teaspoon salt
⅛ teaspoon pepper
Few drops onion juice
¼ cup hot water
½ cup cracker crumbs = 4 crackers, ½ cup stale bread crumbs
¼ cup melted butter

Mix ingredients in order given

***

Stuffed Hearts with Vegetables
Clean and wash calves' hearts, stuff, skewer into shape, lard, season with salt and pepper, dredge with flour, and sauté in pork fat, adding to fat one stalk celery, one tablespoon chopped onion, two sprigs parsley, four slices carrot cut in pieces, half the quantity of turnip, a bit of bay leaf, two cloves, and one-fourth teaspoon peppercorns. Turn hearts occasionally until well browned, then add one and one-half cups Brown Stock, cover, and cook slowly one and one-half hours. Serve with cooked carrots and turnips cut in strips or fancy shapes.[66]

We can probably assume the stuffing mentioned in the first sentence of Stuffed Hearts with Vegetables is also Fish Stuffing I.

Similarly, the 1957 edition of the ever-popular *Joy of Cooking* by Irma S. Rombauer, first published in 1931, also contained recipes for sweetbreads, calves' heads tripe, oxtails, tongue and beef heart, in Rombauer's specific style:

BAKED HEART
Wash:
A beef heart*
Soak it in cold water for 1 hour. Cut away the hard parts. Dry the heart.
Fill it with:
2 cups Bread Stuffing** (page 370)
Tie it with a string. Place it in a casserole. Pour around it:
2 cups diluted canned tomato soup or Stock or Stock Substitute (page 38)
Cover it with:
4 strips of bacon
Cover the dish and bake the heart in a moderate oven 325 from 2 to 3 hours
or until tender. Drain it. Thicken the stock with:
Flour (see Gravy, page 378)
* 2 veal hearts may be substituted.
** Or, you may use as a stuffing:
2 tablespoons onions
2 tablespoons green pepper, chopped
Brown them in:
2 tablespoons butter
and add them to:
2 cups boiled, seasoned rice[67]

These types of recipes had been removed from these two cookbooks by the 1970s and 1980s and are not included in current editions. Jennifer McLagan discusses both of these books in the introduction to her *Odd Bits: How to Cook the Rest of the Animal* and includes more history:

But what about North America? It's true that there is more squeamishness around eating odd bits on this continent than elsewhere, despite strong culinary traditions of using the odd bits. Native Americans ate the entire animal, and early colonists could not afford to waste any part of the animal they slaughtered. As the West opened up, son-of-a-bitch stew and bone marrow, called prairie butter, were common dishes. Buffalo tongues became a delicacy featured on restaurant menus along with ox heart, pig's feet and kidneys....Our growing distaste for linking the meat we cook with the animal it came from has badly hurt odd bits' popularity: some odd bits, like the head, tongue, or heart, instantly remind shoppers they are buying a part of a dead animal—something the dismembered, plastic-wrapped supermarket neat does not do. With loss of knowledge and no one to guide us, we turn for help to the new "experts": the government, meat processors, nutritionists, and even celebrities, and we rely on the health and nutrition claims on the package to make our choices.[68]

Meanwhile our daughter, who's twenty-six at the time of this writing and who enjoyed her first fried alligator at the age of nine at my urging, recently told me about a wonderful seafood boil restaurant in Toledo, Ohio, and how she could eat its crawfish all day long. "I don't know why they say to suck everything out of the head," she told me, "There's nothing in there."

But she doesn't like cornbread. I can't get her to try different versions at all. Go figure.

THE FLINT CONEY COMES TOGETHER

Brayan also got together with master sausage maker Albert Koegel to develop a coney dog that wouldn't burn when kept for a length of time on a relatively hot restaurant flattop grill. Koegel removed the nonfat dry milk and sugars from Koegel's popular Vienna (a version of the Frankfurter Würstel), which Koegel had offered since 1917.[69] Koegel also changed the proportion of ingredients so they contained more fat pork than beef and made the new coney dog somewhat slimmer.[70] There was no indicated change in the casing, as they both use lamb.

The natural lamb-encased Koegel's Coney Frank with the perfect "snap" was born.

Just what does a Koegel's Coney Frank consist of? From the "Products" page on the Koegel Meats website:

Item: Coneys...Description: This is a blend of pork, beef and our unique spices stuffed into a natural casing and then smoked using natural hardwoods. We change the ingredients just a little from our Viennas so that the product can be held on a grill for an extended period of time.... Ingredients: Beef, Pork, Water, Salt, Spices, Sugar, Sodium Citrate,

The interior of the Koegel's Meat store with sawdust on the floor, and meats and sausages displayed in the store cases. The sign at the back reads "A. Koegel & Co." *Courtesy of the Sloan Museum Archives.*

Koegel Vienna, circa 1916

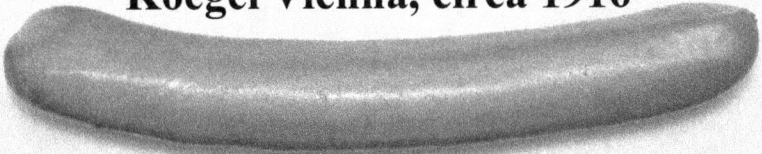

Koegel Coney Frank, circa 1925

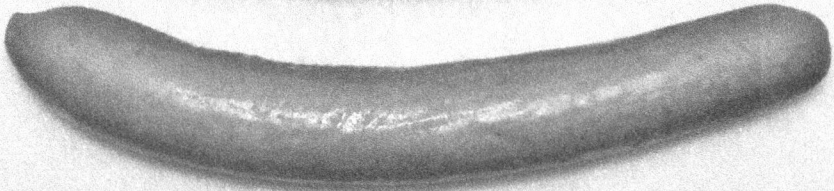

A comparison of Koegel's Vienna for retail sale to consumers and the later Coney Frank for restaurant use, which was derived from the Vienna. *Author collection.*

Dextrose, Sodium Diacetate, Nonfat Dry Milk, Sodium Erythorbate, Spice Extractives, Sodium Nitrite, Garlic, stuffed into lamb casing.[71]

The buns were an issue unto themselves, as they changed often. Initially, they were made by local bakeries.[72] As Macedonians strongly supported one another's businesses, it's possible, even likely, that the buns were made at either the Balkan Bakery, which started on Michigan Avenue before moving to St. John Street, then to Dayton Street after a fire gutted the St. John Street building, or the Universal Bakery on Central Avenue (aka the "Central Bakery").[73] Later on, the buns generally came from the larger commercial Tastee Bakery.[74]

There is one other noteworthy individual in all of this. Sheep rancher George Brown had relocated to Flint from Montana, opening his restaurant at 202 Saginaw Street in 1919. (Neither the 1922 nor the 1925 Flint City Directories show a name for that restaurant, only that George Brown was

The first restaurant in 1922 at this location, 202 South Saginaw, was called George Brown Restaurant. In 1925, it became known as Flint Coney Island. In 1932, the address number was changed to 208. *Courtesy of the Sloan Museum Archives.*

the owner.)[75] In 1925, Brown changed the name of his restaurant to Flint Coney Island, with Simion Brayan and his cousin Paul Branoff, along with Steve George and George Branoff, as partners.[76]

The earlier discussion of the names Brayan, Branoff, and Brown causes me to consider that George Brown may have been a cousin of the other Macedonians who had immigrated to Flint. While unclear from known documentation, it's certainly a possibility.

The rather unassuming Flint Coney Island was open twenty-four hours a day, seven days a week. But almost instantly, the popularity of the restaurant's favorite dish would grow quite large beyond this small Coney Island joint in ways no one ever expected.

WHAT IS A "CONEY ISLAND"?

Online discussions can become rather heated when discussing what defines a *coney*. The most prominent misconception is that it's a hot dog in a bun with a sauce. But history, including the history of the Flint coney, shows that the coney dogs themselves are the defining factor, without the sauce. While the Koegel Coney Frank might be thought of as a "frank made for coneys," it and similar products around the country have historically been packaged using only the word *coney*. The coney is the dog itself, without the sauce, regardless of claims to the contrary.

So then, what defines a *Coney Island* or a *coney dog*, and what differentiates that from a *chili dog*? Is a Detroit coney a chili dog because its sauce has a more wet consistency than the sauce for a Flint coney? Not at all. The term *Coney Island* when referring to the end product is where culture comes into play. A Coney Island restaurant has traditionally been either owned or founded by those of Macedonian, Greek or, more recently, Albanian descent. The coney those restaurants were initially created to serve has been a frankfurter or Vienna-style sausage with a lamb or sheep casing. The sauce, at least in the three main styles in Michigan (Jackson, Detroit and Flint) has at some point been created using beef heart, although that's no longer true for some older styles outside of Flint. In other parts of the country, Coney Island sauces are made with ground beef, but they're also still rather savory like the styles in Michigan.

There's one other term to discuss, that of the *Michigan dog* served in Upstate New York. It was apparently developed in 1927 by Eula and Garth Otis in

Plattsburgh, New York, who had moved to that area from Michigan.[77] With the originators not referring to the dish as a Coney Island, the name itself clearly differentiates it as a chili dog, even though it's traditionally served with a Feltman-style red hot with its natural casing. The Michigan dog's juicy and sweet sauce is also a bit odd to someone like myself who grew up with the Flint coney, even though I'll still enjoy a Michigan dog when given the opportunity.

3

SUCCESS AND COMPETITION

*T*he salesman from Armour who encouraged Albert Koegel to relocate to Flint prior to 1916 had more vision than he probably realized at the time.[78] In 1929, the Flint Chamber of Commerce published a small pamphlet, *Progressive Flint*, which set out specific indicators of what had happened economically in the city since 1910. According to the pamphlet, the population of Flint in 1910 was 38,550 and had grown to 148,800 by 1928, with an estimate of 163,000 for 1930. General Motors was founded in 1908, and its growth through those years had been rather extreme. The average annual wage for Michigan's eleven largest cities was $1,450, but in Flint that average annual wage was $1,780. The number of building permits from 1925 to 1928 alone was more than 28,000, with a total building cost of $63 million. Those four years also saw the construction of 8,000 single-family homes, along with churches and schools. Hurley Hospital was founded during that time, the 6,500-seat I.M.A. Auditorium was built and the 20,000-seat Atwood Stadium was under construction.[79]

The 1929 pamphlet from the Flint Chamber of Commerce didn't mention restaurants, but there was a detailed paragraph that broke down the more than 1,700 retailers in Flint at the time. A *Fact List* showed that 504 grocers and 32 meat markets were located in Flint. Two of those meat markets would have been Koegel's and Abbott's Meats. At the time of the pamphlet's publication, there was one coney shop, Flint Coney Island, located on South Saginaw Street between the two rail lines. The incredible growth of the city would rapidly increase the number of Flint coney shops downtown.[80]

PUBLIC ACCEPTANCE

Flint Coney Island was an almost immediate success. Simion Brayan once stated that they would sell as many as four thousand coneys per day at $0.10 each.[81] If we settle on an average of three thousand coneys per day for a week, that would have brought in approximately $2,100 per week in gross sales.

From the beginning, Flint Coney Island was constantly open, twenty-four hours each day, seven days every week. Grill cooks and waiters worked the same hours as sailors on a ship, twelve hours every day, with no days off. The railroads ran just south of the Flint River, and the stations were just a couple blocks west, within walking distance of the restaurant. Passengers and railroad workers alike discovered the Flint Coney Island as a quick place for a good meal. The workers lived on the second floor of the building, so when the restaurant had a rush, it was possible to grab a broom or mop downstairs and use the handle to bang on the ceiling to call for more workers.[82]

The restaurant workers' meals were included, their rooms were provided and they received $21 each week.[83] If one follows the math on the rate of pay, that's an annual pay of $1,092, or 60 percent of what the factory workers were making in Flint and as much as 75 percent of what factory workers were making across the state in other cities. When you include the room and board, those wages are even better than they first appear. Theirs were rather good wages, far better percentage-wise than the wages of the "fast food" workers of the late twentieth and early twenty-first centuries.

The reference for the above math becomes suspect in view of a later discussion of bootblacks making $20 annually. *Two to Go* states, "Waiters and grill men were paid $21.00 plus free meals for their 12 hour/7 day a week shifts."[84] The language of this sentence implies a weekly wage. But if it was an annual wage, similar to the bootblacks, it renders the preceding paragragh moot. Which fact is true is currently unknown.

In his *"Melting Pot"* book, Evanoff described Brayan in these words:

> *The patriarch of the family is Simion Brayan. For many years Brayan was a partner in the Original Flint Coney Island at Water and South Saginaw Streets and took part not only as an owner but as probably the fastest worker in the place. I have often watched him from outside through the window and wondered how he could put the ingredients of a coney island together so fast. I noticed for one thing he barely looked up but was constantly a combination of eyes and hands.*[85]

It was during the massive growth of the Flint coney's popularity that Simion and Velicia Brayan's family also grew. Their first son, Boris Simion, was born in 1927, followed by Peter in 1928[86] and Carl in 1931.[87] The family was living at their home at 410 Lyon Street on the east side of the street, just two blocks west of Flint Coney Island, aka "Flint's Original," along with cousin Paul Brown and his wife, who was also named Velicia.[88] By 1940, Paul, who by then had taken the name Branoff, and his wife had moved across the street and a couple houses north to 421 Lyon Street to start their own family.[89] Only Paul and Velicia Branoff's brick bungalow survives at the time of this writing.

An even more striking connection to Boufi was a certain Vangel T. "Angelo" Nicoloff. He gave his birthplace as "Boufi, Florina" for the manifest of the SS *Asia* when he immigrated to the United States, arriving at Ellis Island at the age of sixteen on September 25, 1928. He was listed as joining his father, Anthony, owner of Flint's earlier San Juan Chili Parlour, who of course had also come from Boufi. After arriving in Flint, Angelo worked as a cook and waiter at Brayan's Flint Coney Island and then at the Nite Owl in the 1930s and '40s. He would later be the namesake and fellow founder of an iconic Flint coney restaurant.[90]

WHICH WAS THE FIRST CONEY ISLAND SHOP?

There is constant debate about when and where the Coney Island hot dog was first served. The earliest known year is 1914, with Ft. Wayne's Famous Coney Island Wiener Stand in Fort Wayne, Indiana,[91] and both Todoroff's Original Coney Island and Virginia Coney Island[92] in Jackson, Michigan, opening that year. As specific opening dates for those three locations are not known, and it also being unclear if there are other earlier openings at other locations, the first instance of the Coney Island hot dog is yet unknown and no reliable claim can be made.

A timeline of openings of the earliest Coney Island restaurants in widespread areas of the United States is rather telling:

1914 Ft. Wayne Coney Island, Fort Wayne, Indiana
1914 Todoroff's Original Coney Island, Jackson, Michigan (closed 2008)
1914 Virginia Coney Island, Jackson, Michigan
1915 Coney Island Kalamazoo, Kalamazoo, Michigan

1916 Coney Island Lunch, McKeesport, Pennsylvania (closed 2017)
1917 American Coney Island, Detroit, Michigan
1918 Lafayette Coney Island, Detroit, Michigan
1921 Red Hot's Coney Island, Highland Park, Michigan (closed 2021)
1921 Original Coney Island, Duluth, Minnesota (closed 2017)
1922 Empress Chili, Cincinnati, Ohio (While not specifically termed a
       "Coney Island," the Macedonian roots and culture are uniquely
       similar to other coney shops of the time.)
1923 James Coney Island, Houston, Texas
1925 Flint's Original Coney Island, Flint, Michigan (closed 1979)
1926 Coney Island Hot Wieners, Tulsa, Oklahoma (Founder and Greek
       immigrant Christ Economou opened Coney Island Lunch in
       McKeesport, Pennsylvania, ten years earlier, which closed in 2017.
       Coney Island Hot Wieners in Tulsa was his twenty-seventh coney
       shop and his first in Oklahoma.)
1928 Coney Island Deluxe, Duluth, Minnesota

Except for Lafayette and American Coney Islands in Detroit, and Todoroff's Original and Virginia Coney Islands in Jackson, Michigan, each of the owners would likely not have known what the others were doing, as communication between immigrants in those days was sparse. It's also clear that the owners immigrated from various parts of Greece and Macedonia at various times. That the Coney Island phenomenon occurred at all is an interesting matter.

There is no evidence to suggest the earlier Coney Islands in Jackson, Michigan; Fort Wayne, Indiana; or Detroit were the inspiration for later Coney Islands in other areas or that the style of any of these restaurants evolved into any of the other styles. The Coney Island resort area in New York City and its style of hot dog, which resulted in the term "Coney Island hot dog" or "coney dog," is the only known common connection between the Greek Coney Island restaurants.

In a *Metro Times* interview, John Koegel specifically stated, "Beef hearts are in our Koegel Detroit-style chili. National and Leo's Coney Island and Kerby's Coney Island use beef-heart products, though not ours."[93] The other style of coney dog in Jackson, developed by George Todoroff in 1914, has a slightly different history. In a piece by MLive's Brad Flory, Richard Todoroff stated beef heart wasn't in the original recipe. However, he followed this by saying, "Coney restaurants in Jackson began using ground heart during World War II because it was easier to obtain than regular ground beef."[94]

FROM BOOTBLACKS TO CONEYS

Another national phenomenon that occurred in the late 1800s and early 1900s was the prevalence of Greek-owned and operated shoeshine or "bootblack" parlors. In a time of handmade and sometimes high-top boots and shoes that required regular care for daily use, the bootblacks had a continuous source of customers. There were at least a dozen of these parlors in many of the cities the Greeks and Macedonians settled in. A survey of Greek-owned businesses in Manhattan completed in 1909 found 151 shoeshine parlors in that area alone. Greek boys and young men immigrating to America could easily find work at many of these parlors in return for the payment for passage, but it was a hard life of indenture. They would work the sixteen hours each day the shop was open, with no days off, for no more than twenty dollars annually, if the young man was paid at all. The owner-masters, referred to as padrones, did their best to prevent their charges from finding out that walking away from the shoeshine parlor was a real option. The businesses went on for decades, tapering off as men's fashions changed.[95] This further illustrates how Greek and Macedonian

The Mad Hatter bootblack and hat shop, at 200 South Saginaw next to Brayan's Flint Original Coney Island. Opened in 1920, the Mad Hatter is still open today at 424 Saginaw Street. *Courtesy of the Sloan Museum Archives.*

The Koegel Meat Factory started in 1916 at 116 West Kearsley. In 1934, it moved to 217–19 Stevens Street. *Courtesy of the Sloan Museum Archives.*

Tasty Coney Island on South Saginaw Street, owned by Gust and Harry Yeotis. *Courtesy of the Sloan Museum Archives.*

immigration brought complete families to the United States over a period of years and even decades, establishing businesses with a built-in longevity.

Gust Yeotis immigrated to Flint from Greece by way of Traverse City and Cadillac, leaving behind a small string of shoeshine parlors in those cities. He then headed back to Greece in 1929 to marry his wife, Georgia. He would later return to Michigan and settle in Flint.[96]

In 1932, Koegel's built and opened its first standalone processing plant at 217 Stevens Street, closing the retail location at 116 West Kearsley.[97] Since that time, many have urged the Koegel family to get back into retail store operation, but the family has refrained from doing so.

Flint's Original had been the city's only coney shop for only a few years. The first of Brayan's competitors to open was the New System Coney Island in 1929, owned by George Pappadakis, George J. Pappadakis and Michael Pappas, with the U.S. Coney Island opening in 1935. When Gust Yeotis returned from Greece, he and his brother Harry opened Tasty Coney Island in 1938.[98] These were only the first of a steady stream of coney shops to open in Flint.

THE KAFENION AS INSPIRATION

One of the more important aspects of Greece and Macedonia for the story of the Flint coney, and Greek diners in general in the United States, is the existence of the *kafenion* or Greek café or pub in those older cultures. Kafenions still exist today in those regions, operating as they always have. There are tables both inside and outside on the front sidewalk or porch area. They offer Greek coffee, along with beer, brandy and ouzo, a popular anise-flavored aperitif first bottled in the mid-nineteenth century that's considered a suitable replacement for absinthe. A mezze or appetizer of olives and feta (possibly even homemade) might also be served. The kafenion might also include a small grocery area and maybe a bakery or small cooking area. But even more telling concerning its importance, the kafenion was also the post office for the entire village. And as technology progressed into the twentieth century, the kafenion was the location for the village's only telephone.[99]

Even the smallest villages in the Florina prefecture have a kafenion, while larger villages and cities might have a number of them, with a kafenion in each neighborhood or settlement area. The men of the village gathered there to talk about work, politics or whatever else they needed to discuss, argue, or socialize about. Women weren't specifically prohibited from the kafenion, but traditionally only men were patrons.[100]

In an article published in the *New York Times* on April 14, 1996, *Times* writer Edward Lewine examined the connection between the "kaffenion" [sic] and the Greek diner in the United States. Lewine had talked with Dan Georgakas, who later became professor and director of the Greek American Studies Project at the Center for Byzantine and Modern Greek Studies at Queens College and was the author of *My Detroit: Growing Up Greek American in Motor City*. As Georgakas explained to Lewine, the kafenion was definitely the inspiration for the Greek diner, which then also applies to Coney Island restaurants:

> *The Greek diner, Mr. Georgakas said, is an accident of history that makes sense in light of the Greeks who settled here....Many worked their first American jobs in a kaffenion* [sic]—*or found jobs while drinking in one. Such jobs were plentiful and easy to get and soon the immigrants found themselves opening their own restaurant.*[101]

These old country concepts were as important to Simion Brayan in Flint as they were elsewhere in the country. And as more Greeks arrived in Flint and the desire for personal kafenions grew, that's when the Flint coney expanded.

POP, BEER AND WINE

It's often said that the correct beverage to have with a Flint coney is a Vernors Ginger Ale, and nothing else will do. But when looking at images of the coney shops in Flint, along with looking at some of the history of Vernors, we find that wasn't always the case.

The history of the availability of Vernors Ginger Ale in Flint is part of why the product wouldn't have been the first choice for the Flint coney in the early decades of its history. The beverage company opened its Vernors Sandwich Shop at 800 South Saginaw Street in Flint in 1929. (The name Vernors once contained an apostrophe but no longer does.) The Vernors Sandwich Shop stored the barrels of specially made syrup from the Detroit plant in a nearby warehouse, as well as in a tunnel connecting the two buildings. The soda jerks then made each serving of Vernors ginger ale to order, using the specific carbonation required and provided by the company. Vernors didn't begin bottling its product until its first Woodward Avenue bottling plant was completed in 1941. The Vernors Sandwich Shop building was subsequently purchased by Halo Burger in 1951, shortly after the Sandwich Shop closed. So it wasn't until the early 1940s, possibly even the 1950s after the Sandwich Shop closed, that Vernors would have even been available to Brayan for his Flint coney shop.[102]

The question then becomes this: What was Brayan serving for pop? Signage on the Flint Coney Island building indicates Brayan offered pop products from the local M&S Bottling company on Eighth Street, which was founded in 1918. Brayan's offerings would have included M&S flavors such as strawberry-cherry, grape and lime, along with 7 Up and Hires Root Beer and, during World War II, Dr Pepper.[103]

Many photos of Brayan's Flint Coney Island show the words "Beer and Wine" across the bottom of the front of the establishment, and "BEER" in large letters vertically in two places at the top of the three-story building at the rear. But when Brayan opened the restaurant in 1925, these offerings wouldn't have been legal, as Genesee County was known to be dry beginning seven years prior to Prohibition. Those photos would have to be from May 1934 or later.

Genesee County voted to be a dry county via Act No. 381 of the Public Acts of 1913.[104] The State of Michigan outlawed liquor in 1917 with the enforcement of the Damon Act, which was repealed in 1919.[105] Prohibition at the federal level then began on January 17, 1920, and was subsequently repealed on December 5, 1933. Older breweries in Flint, such as Flint Hill Brewing at 2001 South Saginaw Street and Ph. Kling Brewing Co. at 1521 St. John Street, are said to have been shut down by Prohibition in 1920. However, this would have actually occurred in 1913 with Act No. 381 of the Public Acts of 1913.[106] The result was that the county was legally dry for twenty years during some the area's strongest growth.

Following Prohibition, Flint saw its first legal beer on May 11, 1934, the same day as the rest of the state. (References have this date as May 11, 1933, but Prohibition wasn't repealed until December 1933.)[107]

Brayan would have likely bought locally. The brewery at 1521 St. John Street in Flint started small as Dailey Brewing, later becoming the Ph. Kling Brewing Co., brewing D.R. Premier Beer and the Kling's labels such as Kling's Bock Beer and Kling's Bohemian, Lager and Premier Beers. The Flint Hill Brewing Co. at 2001 South Saginaw Street offered its own Bohemia and Bock Beers and King's Tavern Ale, King's Tavern Beer, Schuper Fine

Lager Beer and Viking Royal Lager Beer. The brewery then became White Seal Brewing, offering multiple White Seal–labeled products, including a "Keg-O-Beer," before becoming Valley Brewing Co., offering Heidelberg Pilsener Beer and Michigan Club Pilsener Beer.[108]

The city of Frankenmuth would have also been an excellent local source for beer. Frankenmuth Brewing Co. at 907/926 South Main Street had a number of German-style brews, including Munchner, Bock, Stolz and ales, along with some old English varieties. When the International Ales company took over the brewery, its Iroquois was added to the Frankenmuth line. Later, when Carling moved into the same building, it offered Red Cap Ale and the popular Carling Black Label. Not to be outdone, for a few years after Prohibition ended, the Geyer Bros. Brewing Co. at 415/425 South Main offered its own Frankenmuth beers, ales and lagers.[109]

Rounding out the beer choices in Flint were the ever-popular Budweiser line out of St. Louis, Magnum (brewed by Miller in Milwaukee), Drewry's Ltd (South Bend, Indiana, where they also made a root beer), Goebel (Detroit), Jos. Schlitz Brewing Co. (Milwaukee), Pabst Blue Ribbon (Pabst Brewing, Milwaukee) and Pfeiffer (Detroit).

There were certainly fewer wine choices for a while after Prohibition ended. Michigan wines were made with Concord grapes and weren't as popular as wines from out of state. A state law targeting out-of-state wines with a fifty-cent-per-gallon tax in 1937 solved that issue to some extent. La Salle Wines and Champagne in Detroit, founded in late 1933 by Canadian expatriates, purchased grapes from Lawton-area vineyards like most wineries did to make ports, Concords, Muscatels, Burgundies and dark and white wines, along with fancier selections. The winery added warehouse distribution in 1939, including a warehouse in Flint, so it's possible the La Salle wines were some of Brayan's selections. Other post-Prohibition Michigan wineries were the venerable St. Julian Wines, Bronte Champagne and Wines, the Risdon label from Frontenac Winery, the Houppert Wine Co., the Michigan Winery/Warner Vineyards (which later acquired Houppert), the Paw Paw Wine Co., Milan Wineries and the Lapeer Winery. Some of the wineries banded together to form the Michigan Wine Institute in 1938 for lobbying purposes at the state level, which was quite successful.[110]

MORE COMPETITION

The latter part of the 1930s turned out to be a banner time for the Flint coney itself—though not so much for Flint's Original. Other owners of shoeshine parlors followed the lead of Brayan's earliest competitors, and the popularity of the Flint coneys grew. In the downtown area alone, there were seven Coney Islands by the late 1930s, compared to zero in 1925.[111]

As the popularity of the Flint coney grew, and as other competition opened their doors to a waiting public, other meat companies besides Koegel's and Abbott's attempted to get in on the coney business. This has likely happened countless times over the decades, so much so that it's simply impossible to track. It's not clear how many there were exactly or even how many had made sales attempts. But both the Koegel Coney Frank and Abbott's sauce base have specific characteristics pertaining to performance in the kitchen, and even more so, how the final product presents to the customers in its texture and flavor profile.

By nature, Mediterranean families are extremely close. As the number of restaurants owned and operated by Greeks and Macedonians grew through the early half of the 1900s, a sort of pyramid structure emerged that was similar to how the kafenions operated. Originators of various styles found themselves training siblings, cousins and other family members, who would then establish their own restaurants for their own families to operate. As had occurred with both Brayan's family and the Yeotis brothers, other family members were sent for from their war-torn homeland for a better life and a better future for their entire family.[112]

PERSONAL SUCCESSES

When it came to competition between the Macedonian and Greek Flint coney operators, neither Koegel nor Abbott seemed to want any part of it. Instead, they seemed to be more interested in developing a sense of community among the immigrants and in helping other immigrants fit into their new home. In fact, Tom Yeotis quoted Albert Koegel telling the operator and workers, "We're all immigrants in this together."

Gust's brother Harry Yeotis is a prime example of how well the hot dog slingers were doing. Harry donated $25,000 as a sponsor of the Flint College and Cultural Center and helped with the major fundraising for the construction of Flint's first Greek Orthodox church, located on Beecher Road. He then also began also sending money back to the village of Skortsinos in Greece, where he and Gust were raised. The funds were used to replace the school, which had been destroyed during World War II; for construction of a seven-mile road to the nearest highway; and for a new town hall. Greece's King Paul I decorated Harry twice, and after Harry's passing in 1964, the villagers cast a bronze bust of him and erected it in front of the school, where it still stands today.[113]

THE 1947 FLOOD

While it's unclear exactly when the façade of Flint Original Coney was remodeled, it's quite likely damage from flooding in the 1940s was the reason it occurred. With the Flint River running through it, downtown Flint ended up being prone to regular flooding. Floods occurred in 1904 and 1916, with the 1904 flood being the worst of its time, the waters rising eighty-seven inches in forty-eight hours. After smaller floods in 1941 and 1943, there was then a massive blizzard in March 1946, powerful enough to derail the No. 718 steam locomotive of the Pere Marquette line, as shown in a *Flint Journal* photo. The resulting snowmelt, along with a particularly heavy rainstorm, again caused the downtown area to flood along the river. Other *Journal* images separately show the U.S. Coney Island and Flint Coney Island in the middle of this, the worst flooding Flint has ever seen.[114]

Specific measurements of the floodwaters were published on the front page of the *Flint Journal* on April 6, 1947:

> *The 1941 record of water reaching 55 inches above the intake pipe at the water pumpage station was smashed at 6 p.m. Saturday when it reached 58½ inches above after climbing 5 inches in an hour. It then climbed gradually to 68 inches above at 8 p.m. where it held at 9 p.m., then advanced to 72 inches at 10, 74 inches at 11, 76 at midnight, and 78 at 1 a.m. today.*

The devastation cut a swath about one thousand feet wide that went on for miles. With the water cresting more than one hundred inches above flood stage, several people drowned and more than four hundred residences were severely damaged by the waters. Damage was estimated

1925 to 1940s   1940s to 1979

FLINT CONEY ISLAND
202 / 208 S. SAGINAW ST.

The two façades of Flint Coney Island. *Author collection.*

at the time to be $10 million. The city would experience a milder flood again in 1948. Later efforts at flood abatement proved successful, and Flint hasn't seen flooding on those levels since.[115]

4
SECOND-GENERATION CONEY SHOPS

ANGELO'S, CIRCA 1949

The Dort Motor Car Co. built its version of the automobile from 1915 until 1924 in a facility near the intersection of Davison Road and M54, which became Dort Highway in August 1926. AC Spark Plug purchased the facility in 1925 and over the decades expanded to create a massive complex all the way to Center Road. There, the company manufactured the automotive parts that would be later manufactured under the AC-Delco moniker.[116]

As patrons began developing loyalties to certain styles of Brayan's sauce and to certain owners, some of the earlier Coney Islands to open in downtown Flint ended up closing within about a decade of opening. San Juan Chili Parlor closed in 1945, followed by Famous Coney Island in 1947, with the second U.S. Coney Island location closing in 1952. But following the closing of the San Juan Chili Parlor, the Nicoloffs headed east of Flint to open their next venture.

In 1949, Angelo's Coney Island opened at the intersection of Davison and Franklin Roads, less than a mile from AC Spark Plug, at the location of the former Post Office Coney Island. Ask people today who have eaten at Angelo's who he was, and they'll name Angelo Branoff. But history shows the "Angelo" in the name of the restaurant was owner Vangel "Angelo" T. Nicoloff, who was joined in ownership by Carl Paul; Angelo Popoff; and Tom W., Tom V. and Angelo Branoff were co-owners. Angelo Nicoloff had also worked for Simion Brayan at the original Flint Coney Island for a time before founding Angelo's a full twenty-five years after Brayan first opened his restaurant downtown.[117]

All of the Coney Islands in Flint at the time were open 24/7, and Angelo's was no exception. And as the nearby AC Spark Plug expanded its physical plant and product offerings, business at Angelo's also expanded. A number of separate expansions of the restaurant took it in stages from a small diner of nine stools and ten booths to a 140-seat dining area in multiple rooms sometime in the 1970s, with five cooks running the cookline during lunch.[118]

Even though it had opened twenty-five years after Brayan's Flint Coney Island restaurant and its namesake had also trained and worked there, Angelo's later became one of the restaurants that fell under the public assumption of being "the original Flint coney restaurant." While the actual cause of this myth will likely never be determined, it could be that the size of the restaurant alone and the amount of business it saw were factors in the perpetration of this rumor. Of course, it could also be later signage at the restaurant itself touting it as being "home of the real original." Regardless of the reason, the folklore remains today. Business was booming, and there was no end in sight.

MODERNIZATIONS

In an odd twist of events, back on the other side of Lake Michigan, Plankinton, Armour and Co., where Albert Koegel had worked, had indirectly become Cudahy Packing, which Edward Abbott had worked for. In about 1955, Cudahy Packing purchased the Twin City Packing plant Albert Koegel had supervised north of Milwaukee, combining the two men's meatpacking origins. For reasons unknown at this time, Albert Koegel's former Twin Cities Packing plant closed approximately five years later.[119]

The overall physical and economic atmosphere in downtown Flint and across the country changed in the 1940s and '50s as railways made the transition from steam to diesel locomotives. The first U.S. diesel operating on a mainline occurred in 1934 when both the Union Pacific and Burlington Railroad began passenger service using the locomotives. The overall transition didn't take much time: Grand Trunk operated one of the last steam locomotives, which made its final run on September 20, 1961, only twenty-seven years after that first diesel mainline began operation.

The Coney Island restaurant was one of many of diner-style restaurants that developed in the late nineteenth and early twentieth centuries. The 1950s and '60s saw a massive increase in the number of chain-owned and franchised fast-food restaurants throughout the United States. This caused a similar decline in the number of family-owned diners in metropolitan areas first, spreading to rural areas later. Popular designs based on a 1955 Kullman Dining Car design provided counter and table service in the style of the California coffee shop, which copied aspects from up-and-coming chains such as Denny's and Howard Johnson's. The owners of diner-style restaurants, and ultimately Coney Island restaurants, modified their look and operation in attempts to remain relevant.[120]

As time went on, some Coney Islands expanded their menus. Images of some of the menus from the various Coney Islands in the area have floated around the internet for a few years. An Angelo's menu from the early 1990s (dating being based on the Pepsi logo design in the center) contained the following items and prices, as posted:

Hamburg Steak	4.75
Roast Beef	4.75
Baked Ham	4.75
Hot Sandwich	4.00
Franks & Beans	3.00
Ham & Potatoes	2.50
Chef Salad	2.70 & 3.70
Grilled Ham & Cheese	2.60
Grilled Cheese	1.45
Sausage Sandwich	2.00
Warm Sandwich	2.50
Meat & Egg	2.55
Egg Sandwich	1.40
BLT	2.30
Chili	1.70
Soup	1.45
Cottage Cheese Salad	1.40
American & French Fries	1.45
Hamburg	1.45 DX 1.60
Cheeseburg	1.50 DX 1.70
Coney Island	1.45

1 Egg	1.75 W Meat 2.90
2 Eggs	2.10 W Meat 3.20

Omelets

Cheese	2.90
Ham & Cheese	3.90
Western	4.20
Ham	3.30
Coffee & Tea	.90
Juice	.90
Milk	.50 & 1.20
Pop	.80 & .90
Malts	1.45

Soups

Monday	Vegetable Beef
Tuesday	Chicken Noodle
Wednesday	Beef Noodle
Thursday	Beef Barley
Friday	Pea
Saturday	Vegetable Beef

In Edward Lewine's *New York Times* article of April 14, 1996, James L. Dontis of Dontis Produce is quoted as saying, "In the 1960's, in response to the fast-food boom, diners frantically added items to their menus, which often go on for page after page....The familiar interior design, including booths and Formica-topped counters and tables, came in around the same time."[121]

OLDER VERSUS NEWER GREEK CONEY ISLANDS

Newer Coney Island restaurants in Flint followed the trend described by Lewine, moving away from the lunchroom-style restaurant design that had been prevalent in the local Coney Island joints. Menus were also expanded to include many staples of the diners they emulated, resulting in family restaurants that served full breakfast, lunch and dinner menus. Starlite Coney Island was one of these newer breed of Coney Island, as were Venus on Fenton Road, Atlas on Corunna Road and many others. Anastosios

"Alex" Popoff, who was born in Boufi on November 5, 1939, and his wife, Magda "Maggie," took over the Starlite Coney Island restaurant in 1968 at the intersection of Davison and Center Roads, farther east of Angelo's location outside the downtown Flint area. Capitol Coney Island on Van Slyke south of Bristol Road was founded the same year.[122] While the sale of coneys isn't the core of these businesses as they were in the earlier heyday of the Flint coney, the newer-style restaurants still attract locals who see the restaurants as "their place." And the Flint coney still features prominently on their menus and in their cultures.[123]

ABOUT "TRADITIONAL" GREEK DISHES

In this work, I use quotation marks when talking about "traditional" Greek dishes. This is because, contrary to popular belief, they're dishes that emerged in the early twentieth century. There's a timeline of events from about 1900 onward when Greek cuisine was redefined in homes, restaurants and around the world. Developments that occurred in the Coney Island restaurants in the United States almost exactly followed what happened in the old country.

The Greek poet Archestratus is largely credited with putting together the first cookbook ever written. He began traveling in about 350 BC and wrote what was considered a humorous poem he called "Hedypatheia," which means "Life of Luxury." Sixty-two fragments of this poem survive and were republished in 1994 and 2011 by John Wilkins and Shaun Hill.[124]

> The courses…were made up of a sitos or carbohydrate element, barley and wheat to fill the stomach and strong flavors or opsa to provide extra proteins and vitamins and interest the palate. These opsa…ranged from the best sea bass to a salad of bitter herbs or cheese and onions. Greedy people might eat too much carbohydrate, luxurious people too many opsa, particularly highly-prized fish.[125]

Fish and meat were the only entrée items included, with the meat being hare:

> [Bring] the roast meat in and serve to everyone while they are drinking, hot, simply sprinkled with salt, taking it from the spit while still a little rare. Do not worry if you see the ichor [blood of the gods] seeping from the meat, but eat greedily.

Archestratus discussed boiling, roasting or grilling and only using light sauces, oils and seasonings. For him, "boiled chickpeas, broad beans, apples, and dried figs" were signs of poverty.[126]

As late as the nineteenth century, and even into the twentieth century, Greek cooking as we know it today didn't exist. There was no moussaka, souvlaki, "Greek salad," stuffed grape leaves or most of the other items seen on today's "Greek" menus. Many areas of the region were rather rural, with people living in poverty, so the majority ate quite rustic foods. They made cheese from sheep's milk and baked numerous kinds of dense breads. They harvested and cooked potatoes (which had only been introduced in the early nineteenth century), grapes, olives, figs and wild greens. There was octopus, herring, skate, grouper and anchovies, all grilled over open flame. And the roast or grilled meat from goats, lamb, chickens, geese, pigs and beef cattle were included in many main dishes, with "nose-to-tail" being a common concept to ensure a butchered animal provided many meals.[127]

It then becomes clear that, when Simion Brayan ate the coney in Rochester, New York, he thought of a better way to make it using the offal of beef heart and kidney. The higher-end Greek dishes Americans think of today weren't developed until later. It's most likely they're still not cooked in the area around Boufi/Akritas even today. Those dishes simply aren't how villagers in the region tend to eat.[128]

This also puts to rest the myth of there being ground hot dogs in original Flint coney sauce. Simion Brayan wouldn't have considered such a thing. He probably wasn't a cook per se: He came from a small village and was a fur dryer for a time when he lived in Toronto until immigrating to the United States that second time in 1921. He would, however, know the dishes he grew up with, and ground hot dogs weren't in that repertoire. He simply would not have used such an ingredient. It then follows that Vangel T. Nicoloff, the namesake of Angelo's who was from the same village of Boufi, wouldn't have used ground hot dogs in his Flint coney sauce either.

So where did the Greek dishes we know today come from? In Greece, the word *tselementes* basically means "cookbook." There's an individual behind that term who introduced the dishes Americans think of when talking about Greek cooking. Nikolaos Constantinus Tselementes was a Greek cook at eateries owned by relatives. He then studied in Vienna and was cooking at various embassies in Athens when he began publishing his *Odigos Mageirikis* (Cooking Guide) periodical in 1910, which included recipes and dietary and nutritional advice. He first immigrated to the United States on December 15, 1920, aboard the *Themistocles*. (His name was misspelled on the manifest as "Tsilimintis, Nikolaos.")[129] While living in the United States, he published his first Greek-language cookbook, which is where he first demonstrated American and European influences in his cooking techniques and ingredients. Returning to Greece in 1930, he began a cooking school whose collection of recipes was reprinted at least nine times. These had the same outside influences as his earlier Greek language cookbook.[130]

On September 28, 1949, Tselementes immigrated to the United States again aboard KLM Royal Dutch Airlines into New York from Amsterdam, listing himself on the manifest as a "Professor of Cookery" and his destination as the St. Moritz Hotel.[131] In 1950, he published his only English-language cookbook, *Greek Cookery*. The book presented multiple versions of moussaka, souvlaki and the rest of the so-called Greek classics, which, in fact, weren't.[132] It also ended up being a return to the "Lifestyle of Luxury" in a manner similar to the dishes outlined by Archestratus, as described by Greek food historian Aglaia Kremezi:

> *For today's Greeks the real moussaka, deliciously flavored with ground lamb, is not an everyday dish. It is baked in urban homes as a treat for guests and family on special festive days. It has a lush topping of bechamel sauce or "cream," as it is often called.*[133]

These were the dishes later Greek immigrants included in their Coney Island menus as they opened newer restaurants beginning in the late 1950s. Those later immigrants grew up with Tselementes's dishes beginning in 1910. The dishes had ended up being a part of their lives, and their menus reflected his influence.

THE OLDER STALWARTS

In stark contrast to Tselementes's influence, the more complex Greek Coney Island menus weren't seen as much in the older coney shops, as again, those founders had never cooked that way. One of the oldest Greek Coney Islands in the country is Fort Wayne's Famous Coney Island. The restaurant opened in 1914, the same year as Todoroff's Original and Virginia Coney Islands in Jackson, Michigan, and was one of the earliest, if not the earliest, Coney Islands in the nation. It was purchased two years later by Macedonian Vasil Eschoff, whose descendants still operate the restaurant today. Even now the menu is extremely simple, offering only its own coney, cheese dog, hamburger, cheeseburger, bowls of chili, baked beans, chips and homemade pie. Beverage selections are fountain and canned pops, coffee, tea, bottled water and milk.[134] At his Flint Original Coney, Brayan was the same way with his even smaller menu, never changing from the original coney, chili and drink selections.[135] Angelo's menu from the 1990s never included the newer "traditional" Greek dishes, nor did the Nickolson's Red Hots Coney Island in Highland Park mentioned earlier, nor the venerable Lafayette Coney Island in downtown Detroit. This specifically illustrates the older coney operators' nonreaction to Tselementes's influences.

A representative post-Tselementes Greek Coney Island menu is listed in Appendix B.

CONEY ISLANDS VERSUS CORPORATIONS AND FRANCHISE OPERATIONS

It's no surprise the Flint Coney Island concept has never lent itself well to corporate takeovers or franchise concepts. There was a failed attempt to unionize the Flint coney workers at about the same time as the sit-down strike of 1936 at General Motors. Of that attempt to organize the coney shop workers, Tom Yeotis of Tasty Coney Island is quoted as saying, "It's tough to organize Greeks. Greeks are very independent."[136] This independence indicates a strong desire to keep things close among friends and family, to do things only in a certain way, to maintain real control over the work that's done to support the family. It explains a lot about how the Coney Islands have developed over the decades as havens and training grounds for family, as well as friends who have become like family. Franchise operations and corporate takeover are hardly conducive to this line of thinking.

The founders of some of the largest corporate-owned franchises had similar feeling about what their family businesses might or did become. In his autobiography, with the hindsight of ten years after selling his Kentucky Fried Chicken franchise concept to a group of investors, Colonel Harland Sanders was quite blunt. Before the sale, he'd run his own franchise operation and was known among his franchisees for his friendship to the point of being treated as family. But the Colonel was also known for unexpectedly coming in and removing his cookers, chicken, spices and other company-related items if the operator didn't toe the line. He couldn't do this after the sale of his company to investors, of course, and seemed to regret having lost not only control of the product but also the family aspect of contact with the franchisees he'd groomed:

> *Many times I've been accused of being a perfectionist. Maybe I am. But I do know how chicken should be fried, and if it's gonna be fried using my special recipe, then it's got to be done right. I don't want nobody foolin' around with their own ideas. If he had my franchise then he had to do it my way....Probably I'm old-fashioned and don't appreciate the ways of big corporations today. The business I developed was a personal one. I knew most all of the franchisees by their first names, and many of them slept in my beds* [at his motel in Corbin, Kentucky] *and ate breakfast at my table. We was just one big family....It would be nice if I could say I didn't care about all of these goings on, but that wouldn't be the truth. My concern is not so much the high financing that seems to be necessary to keep Kentucky Fried Chicken growin' as it is with the kind of people who are out there in their Kentucky Fried Chicken stores a-sellin' it, and then with the high quality of the product itself. That's what made it a success from the start.*[137]

In the late 1960s and early '70s, a few Detroit Coney operators developed Greek Coney Island chain concepts with coney dogs as part of complex post-Tselementes menus. National Coney Island was first in 1965, with Kerby's Koney Island opening a few years later. Kerby's opened a total of about twenty locations in the Detroit suburbs. As time went on, National ended up with twenty stores as well. As they also distributed their sauce and coney dogs through GFS Foodservice, along with being available at the GFS Marketplace stores, they have become the de facto supplier for the Detroit-style coney across Michigan.[138]

Leo's Coney Island was founded in 1972 by Peter and Leo Stassinopoulos with their Southfield Souvlaki Coney Island, but instead of owning all their own Leo's stores, they also have franchising available. They also went further than National and Kerby and in the twenty-first century expanded into Flint and Genesee County. As they purchase products from Koegel's for their menu, the Genesee County locations also offer the Flint coney alongside the Detroit coney they've offered for more than forty years.[139]

Other post-Tselementes Greek restaurant chains exist, although they don't offer a signature coney dog as part of their menus. Kalamata Greek Grill opened in Detroit in 2008 and at the time of this writing has two locations, although they're now open for franchising. Outside of Michigan is Grecian Gyro, which opened in 1982 in Atlanta; Taziki's Mediterranean Café, the largest of the Greek chains having been founded in 1998 and now having a few dozen locations in fifteen states; Little Greek Fresh Grill, founded in 2004 in Florida; Taste of Mediterranean, which also started in 2004 but up in Toronto; the Hungry Greek, which began in 2006 in Florida and is also in Hot Springs, Arkansas; the Simple Greek in Pittsburgh and Chicago; and Opa Life Greek Café/Eatery/Express, which opened in 2014 with the three styles of locations being in Arizona.

ANGELO'S PASSING

The charter founder of the second generation of Flint coney owners, Vangel T. "Angelo" Nicoloff, passed away on April 23, 1969, at the age of fifty-seven. His partners continued to operate Angelo's long after his passing, with multiple owners who were also referred to as "Angelo" being mistaken for Vangel as "the original Angelo."

PALACE CONEY ISLAND—A PERSONAL MECCA

In August 1970, the Genesee Valley Shopping Center opened northeast of the intersection of Linden and Miller Roads, almost eight miles west of Flint's Original.[140] Gus and Angelo Vergos opened the Palace Coney Island in the mall as part of that opening, setting up shop in the eastern wing that was anchored by a Hamady Bros. grocery store.[141] It was soon afterward that this author's family began our Friday evening dinner and shopping tradition. With the size of the Genesee Valley mall, its number of stores and the fact that Hamady Bros. had leased space for a full grocery there, the mall quickly became our go-to place for that tradition. And so it was in late 1970 that I enjoyed my first Flint coney at the age of eight or nine, at the Vergos brothers' Palace Coney Island.

The space was only about twenty-four feet wide but fairly deep. The gate opening was the left twelve feet of the mall entrance, the other twelve feet being a wall with a small window. Through that window you could see Gus or Angelo Vergos manning the grill. He would be placing coney franks from the Koegel's box on the heated flattop grill with his left (nearest to the window into the mall) and then moving them to his right as they cooked, all under the watchful eye of the sign that read, "You are enjoying a Koegel's coney!" You'd pick up a tray and place your order for your coneys.

The cook would then take yours off the end to his right, place the coneys in the steamed buns and top them with Vergos's own Flint coney sauce made from Abbott's base, then stripes of yellow mustard and finally tiny pieces of perfectly minced onions. You would then move your tray to the left to order your sides and drink from other workers behind the service counter, in between the countertop coolers and the pop machine that were all located between you and the workers, then pay at the end at the single cash register. Our family would then take two of the red vinyl booths available throughout the rest of the space to enjoy our meal.

On Friday evenings and Saturdays, the line for Palace Coney Island generally wrapped around that wall at the opening and stretched down the mall corridor. There were probably at least twenty people in that line, increasing to much greater numbers during weekends and holiday seasons.

The migration of businesses to the large, enclosed shopping centers that were being developed in rural areas across the country in the 1970s brought shoppers away from the downtown areas of cities. Businesses in downtown Flint either relocated to the areas surrounding Genesee Valley Mall or Eastland Shopping Center at Center Road and Court Street near AC Spark Plug or into the malls themselves. The coney shops in downtown Flint also lost a lot of their customers, with both U.S. Coney Island locations closing in 1971. Tasty Coney Island had already closed in 1966, the rest had closed prior to that.

By the mid-1970s, Flint's Original was once again the only coney shop in Flint's downtown area.[142]

EXPANSION SETTLES DOWN

Out in Denver in about 1969, John and Helen Bibilikow closed their Scotti's Steakhouse & Pizzeria. Instead of being Greek or Macedonian, John was born in Gradetz, Bulgaria, while Helen was born in Flint. John immigrated to Flint, and they had married in 1957 prior to relocating to Denver. After moving back to Genesee County, they opened Scotti's Coney Island at Belsay and Lapeer Road, where there once was a Seeley's Drug Store.[143] While serving Flint coneys, they became even more famous for their homemade coleslaw and fish and chips made with fresh cod and their own batter. Scotti's Coney Island was quite a popular restaurant, with this author enjoying the fish and chips many times over the years.

In the 1970s, Abbott's Meats moved to Blackington Avenue near the intersection of Corunna Road and Ballenger Highway, where it still operates today. In 1972, Koegel's opened its current processing facility on Bristol Road on one of the industrial pads at Bishop International Airport. The airport opened on October 1, 1934, and had seen many improvements. In 1970, a master plan was developed for the airport, and the deal with Koegel's to move to the new location was one of the results of that plan.[144]

The new 100,000-square-foot Koegel's facility wasn't simply a collection of equipment arranged in a set of production lines. Production moves east–west so there's zero contact between raw and finished product to prevent cross-contamination, with the floor being brick, as acids from production erodes concrete. The facility was also lined with stainless steel to prevent rust.[145]

A future coney operator, David Gillie, had one of his first jobs at Starlite Coney Island in 1973, where he was taught the restaurant's recipe for Flint coney sauce. In an email, Gillie wrote, "They did change the preparation of it while I was there in that they changed from using beef suet to start it, to using vegetable shortening. While I was there, there always was a debate about whether or not to add garlic. The oldest owner of the three would add a bit sometimes, but we never did." Gillie went on to earn a degree in economics from the University of Michigan's Flint campus, but he returned to the Flint coney scene later.

Another unique development had its beginnings in 1976 when John Hoenicke opened his Civic Park Lounge. He was one of the operators making his own Flint coney sauce from scratch, and his wife had begun to freeze some of the sauce for sale to customers to take home. This would prove to be somewhat lucrative in the future.[146]

It's unclear at this time when the Tastee Bakery closed, no longer supplying the coney buns needed for the Flint coney restaurants. In 1977, Mr. Bread was established at Dort Highway and Davison Road by a couple of former bakers of a larger bakery, possibly Tastee Bakery itself. Their first coney customer was Gus Vergos and his Palace Coney Island out at the Genesee Valley Shopping Center. Mr. Bread's Flint's Original Coney Buns, soft seven-inch buns, were also used at Angelo's Coney Island and many other shops.[147]

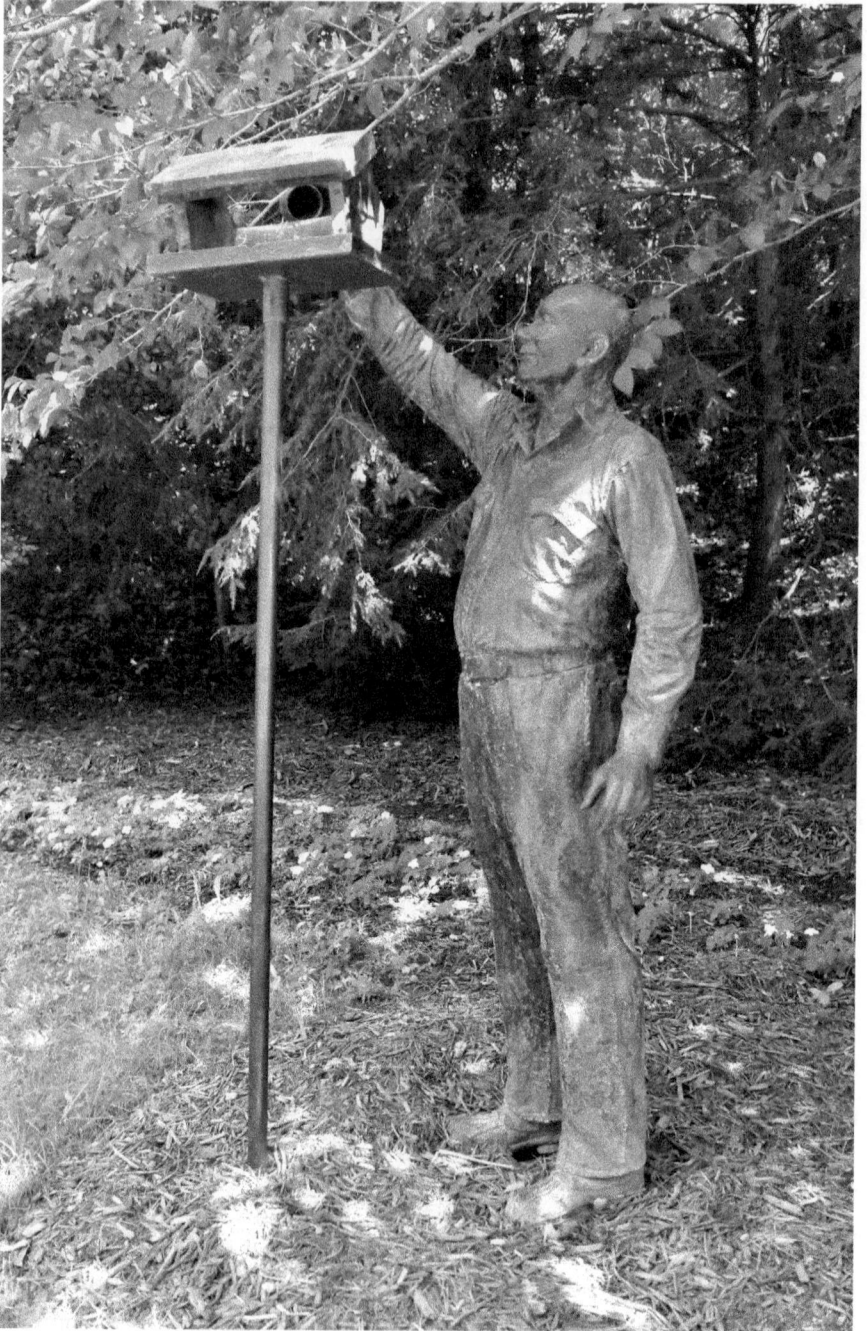

Albert Koegel, "The Provider," just inside the entrance of Sunset Hills Cemetery. *Author collection.*

THE END OF AN ERA

The diesel-powered railroads bypassed the downtown area in the late 1960s, and Amtrak began offering passenger service at a station on the CN/GTW line (GTW being the rerouted Grand Trunk Western line) south of the downtown area on September 15, 1974. All the rail lines on either side of Flint Coney Island were removed in 1976, as was the Pere Marquette rail bridge over the Flint River.[148]

Albert Koegel passed away on August 21, 1975, at the age of ninety. Koegel took an interest in Sunset Hills Cemetery on Flushing Road early on and is buried there. As visitors enter the cemetery, the first sculpture they see is *The Provider* by Derek Wernher, which depicts the elder Albert Koegel lifting a tin can to a bird feeder.

After five decades living in Flint, Simion Brayan's wife, Velicia, passed away on December 27, 1976. Simion closed Flint's Original in 1979 after having been in business serving his coneys in downtown Flint for fifty-five years.

In 1980, a scrap collector was driving by when the building housing Simion Brayan's Flint's Original Coney Island was being demolished. He told the crane operator to put Brayan's blue sign in the back of his pickup truck and stored it in his garage until much later.[149]

Simion and Velicia's daughter Anna S. Brayan Popoff passed away on February 21, 1981, just shy of her seventieth birthday. Simion Brayan, still bright and vibrant in his early nineties and surrounded by friends and family, continued on in his adopted hometown of Flint.

A decade after Simion closed his restaurant, St. Nicholas Orthodox Church on South Center Road in Burton was the site of Simion Brayan's one-hundredth birthday celebration in 1989. He had come a long way and seen a lot, emigrating from a war-torn country, to develop a truly local restaurant staple based on his own Greek heritage, a staple that continues to enjoy a popularity rarely seen. Simion and his partners were quite successful, and he had a proud and loving family, along with hundreds of true friends.

Simion P. Brayan passed away in Flint on July 22, 1990, at the age of one hundred.

5

FURTHER DEVELOPMENTS

THE FOLKLORE OF THE "ANGELO'S" RECIPE WITH GROUND HOT DOGS

Unfortunately for anyone interested in the authenticity of the Flint coney sauce they make at home, a recipe containing ground beef, ground hot dogs and tomato sauce has long been touted as the "original recipe." The original source of this recipe is currently unknown, but it has, in most instances, been attributed to Angelo's Coney Island, which is patently false. The recipe was originally published and then republished in the *Flint Journal*, printed in books and magazines and reposted on the internet more times than can be counted, with stories ranging from "my aunt/uncle/stepdad/mom/second-cousin-twice-removed got this from the owner/former-owner/ex-employee of the original restaurant" to "the original owner's wife allowed this to be published after his death!" The original source of this recipe is still being researched, but the Post Office Coney Island, which as of 1945 preceded Angelo's at its first location, may have been that source.[150]

When asked to assist in finding Joy Gallagher's initial printing of this recipe prior to 1978, Jonathan Kirkwood, a *Flint Journal* archivist at the Sloan Museum, was unable to locate it in December 2020.

A Possible Origin

In March 2016, a few blogs with Flint coney recipes heard from a gentleman by the name of Vaughn Marlowe. Marlowe was eighteen when Angelo's first opened in 1949, working as an assistant window trimmer downtown at Smith-Bridgman's. He was born and raised in Flint "with occasional summers in Canada." What he has to say about what was there before Angelo's began at the intersection of Davison and Franklin is quite interesting. His story indicates the source may have been another Macedonian who was referred to as "Sam," who apparently did use ground hot dogs in his sauce. Here's Marlowe's story:

> *I grew up two blocks away from Angelo's on Arlington, and ate there the day it opened in a new building under that name. The prior name was the Davison Road Coney Island, and it was housed in a red wooden diner-style edifice of dubious construction.* [Note: The 1946 Flint City Directory shows this restaurant as being the "Post Office Coney Island," owned by a John Nichols.[151]] *We spent many an hour playing the pinball machine and the nickel jukebox at that place. My pals and I were not a part of the Lloyd's Drugstore culture across the street because that was for teen couples mostly. We were thirteen-to-fifteen-year-olds without girlfriends at that point, although that changed soon enough on schedule with our hormones....A coney with a cup of coffee was twenty cents. Malts and shakes were the same, a piece of pie a dime. It was possible in 1948 to eat on a dollar a day. My forty-dollars-a-week salary went a long way back then. Sam* [last name unknown], *aka "Silent Sam," used to scrape the grill at night and add bits of hamburger, sausage, bacon, hot dogs and ham to the big pot of constantly simmering hot dog sauce that he would "taste to test" throughout the day. I know; I used to watch him. He was an old-school Macedonian cook and wasted nothing. He even added bits of goat meat leftovers from meals his wife cooked at home. I also remember his liberal use of cumin and paprika. Sam kept an unusually savory kitchen. That was seventy-five years ago, kids.*

When I asked if he thought the Flint coney sauce recipe might have come from "Silent Sam," Marlowe replied in this manner:

> *I know nothing about the recipes. Years later, I made a dry sauce based on some item sent me from the* Journal. *All I know about Sam's was the scrapings and the aroma rich with cumin, onion and paprika. His using meats from the grill, however, was understandable: it's something my frugal grandmothers would have done. (During the 1930s depression my mother would boast that she could get "two meals for three" out of a pound of*

hamburger; in fact she boasted about that up until she died a few years ago at ninety-seven.)...My late sainted mother (aren't they all?) had the last word on the Coney Island hot dog. She came to Flint with her folks from Canada in 1925 and spent the first five days downtown in a hotel near the tracks. She and her brothers and sister lived on burgers and hot dogs from a nearby Coney Island—the "Original," I'm betting—and she remarked before she died that she never lost her taste for them...that's eighty-five years! Incidentally, the dogs from my youth were densely packed and juicy: grilled hot dog dry, sauce, mustard, finely chopped onions, in that unvarying sequence. And they popped! when you took the first bite.

The Recipe's Second Printing

In the 1970s, *Flint Journal* food editor Joy Gallagher was writing a regular column titled "Kitchen Clinic." In her column published on May 23, 1978, Gallagher provided two recipes for "Flint-Style Coney Sauce." Both of these recipes came with supposed claims of being the "original" recipe for Flint-style coney sauce.

Kitchen Clinic
By Joy Gallagher, Journal Food Editor

I hesitate to bring up the subject of Coney Island hot dog sauce, because I know I will get calls and letters telling me I don't have the REAL one.

Maybe so, in fact, I have two—the one that is supposed to be the "original" Coney Island sauce, which I ran some time ago and everyone raves about, and another that came to me recently from a reader who swears it is the sauce served at Angelo's.

I'm not making any claims, I'm only saying that if either of these is not the real thing, they will do dern [sic] well until something better comes along.

It is reasonable to assume that there are differences in the sauces served at the various hot dog establishments around town town. Every chef adds his own touch, and recipes can change over the years as new chefs come and go.

The "original" sauce recipe came to me from a woman who said she was the wife of a chef at the original Coney Island, and that she copied the recipe from his personal recipe book. I believe her. This is the recipe she sent.

"Original" Coney Island Sauce
1 T. butter
1 T. margarine
1½ lbs. lean ground beef
2 med. onions chopped
1 clove garlic, crushed
Salt, pepper to taste.
2 T. chili powder
1 T. prepared mustard
1 6-oz. can tomato paste
1 6-oz. can water
4 or 5 wieners

Combine everything but wieners and simmer over low heat until thick. Grind the wieners and add to sauce. Cook 15 minutes longer. Do not brown ground beef before using.

It seems that some chefs, if the sauce was a little thin, added a few crumbled soda crackers to sauce, but apparently it was not part of the original recipe.

The second recipe uses beef heart, which is an admitted part of the recipe if you talk to some chefs. As I said, it is supposed to be Angelo's recipe, and it came from a trusted source, but you will have to decide for yourself if it tastes just the same.

Coney Island Sauce

1 beef heart
1 lb. hamburger
2½ t. cumino (Mexican spice)
1 t. sugar
2 small onions, chopped fine
2 t. chili powder
1 t. pepper
1 small bottle catsup
4 t. vinegar
2 t. salt

Simmer beef heart in water to cover until tender. Cool, then grind fine. Cook hamburger and onion in heavy skillet or saucepan until hamburger loses its red color and starts to brown. Add remaining ingredients, cover and simmer for one hour, stirring occasionally. If needed, add a small amount of water.[152]

It's interesting to note that the Angelo's statement by Gallagher was for the beef heart recipe. However, in the myth this has always been attributed to the ground hot dog recipe that was printed above the beef heart recipe in this column.

In this particular column, Gallagher used phrases such as "calls and letters telling me I don't have the REAL one," "the one that is supposed to be the 'original' coney island sauce" and more importantly, "I'm not making any claims."

In considering these particular phrases, it is easy to conclude that Gallagher herself didn't believe a word of any of the rumors regarding the ground hot dog recipe. In his book *Scoops: Ron Krueger's Inside Dish on the Flint Journal's Favorite Recipes*, the longtime food writer and Gallagher's successor from May 1989 until June 2011 included the ground hot dog recipe she printed earlier, without a credit listed in Krueger's book.[153] I asked Krueger about this on November 6, 2014, and he replied, "That recipe appeared in the *Journal* several times over the years. Don't think I ever saw it in the context of a story or ever saw any attribution. It always included the word 'original' in the title, but anybody who knows anything knows otherwise."

There's also an important clause in the second paragraph of Gallagher's column of May 23, 1978, regarding the ground hot dog recipe: "the one that is supposed to be the 'original' Coney Island sauce, which I ran some time about and everyone raves about." Obviously, this particular column still isn't the original source of that recipe. An earlier column would be the real public source.

Finally, Gallagher's column of May 23, 1978, is apparently the direct source of the two "Flint-style Coney Sauce" recipes included on the last page of *Two to Go: A Short History of Flint's Coney Island Restaurants* published by the Genesee County Historical Society.[154] While the authors of *Two to Go* didn't quote Gallagher's column directly and included the two recipes themselves without a reference, they are indeed identical to the recipes in that column.

Angelo's Specifically Refutes the Recipe

On April 18, 1995, *Flint Journal* food editor Ron Krueger published a column describing how he had taken the recipe containing ground hot dogs to Tom V. Branoff, one of the owners of Angelo's at the time. In the column, Branoff specifically refuted the claims surrounding the folklore of the ground hot dog recipe, using such phrases as "No ground beef; we use beef heart," and "Yes, some chili powder, but no tomato paste." Krueger then stated, "Anybody who has eaten more than one or two Flint coneys knows there are no ground up wieners in the sauce."[155]

Krueger taking this particular recipe to Branoff belies the fact that Joy Gallagher's claim was that the recipe containing beef heart was supposedly the Angelo's recipe. However, this action does indicate that the rumors that Angelo's recipe contained ground hot dogs had already made the rounds and was building into the current folklore that it is today.

At the end of this column, Krueger specifically took back any of Joy Gallagher's claims about the recipe.

Further Attempts at Debunking the Folklore

It appears Krueger made many attempts over the years to get a handle on and refute the claims of his predecessor about this recipe and the resulting rumors and folklore. Later columns indicate readers were still asking him to print the "original" Flint coney sauce recipe that they'd seen in the *Flint Journal*. He would include the ground hot dog recipe, but not without including his real knowledge that the rumors and folklore were patently untrue. Even though he tried valiantly to get control of the situation, his efforts apparently went unheeded. Readers still seemed to insist Joy Gallagher had been right all along.

In his column of January 6, 1998, Krueger wrote that, in Joy Gallagher's original column, "Neither the name of the 'snitch' nor of the restaurant ever was revealed." About the recipe, he stated that it "was immediately suspect because it contained no beef organ meet, which was part of the 'original' sauce recipe and is still used today." As to the second recipe in Gallagher's column, it "contains beef heart but also ground beef, which isn't in the sauce served at local coney outlets."[156]

THE FLINT CONEY'S PRO BASKETBALL PLAYER

Growing up in Flint in the 1970s was much more difficult than it was earlier in the twentieth century. For most families trying to make it in Flint, going out was a trip to McDonald's. Marty Embry was young, hardworking teenaged basketball player who didn't go to a restaurant until his junior year in high school when his girlfriend Joya took him. He now says he decided to marry her because of that meal, and she remains by his side today.

In 1981, Flint Central High School's basketball team won the state championship. (They would win it again in 1982.) Angelo's co-owner at the time, Angelo Branoff, invited the team to enjoy a meal at the restaurant. Branoff's one stipulation: "Eat as much as you want, but you can't take anything with you when you leave." Embry was one of those players. In an email to me, he recalled that he ate twelve cheeseburgers, six fries, one with every other burger, three strawberry milkshakes "and a coke with every French fry order." Thinking back on that meal he had at Angelo's as a high school basketball player, in late 2014 Embry said, "I couldn't eat that much today if you paid me a million dollars to do it!"

After high school, Embry headed to DePaul University in Chicago and played basketball for four years. He was then drafted by the Utah Jazz, but instead ended up playing as a professional in Europe for thirteen years for countries such as Italy and Spain. He came back to Flint later.

CHANGING OF THE GUARD AT KOEGEL'S

After Koegel's opened its Bristol Road processing plant at Bishop Airport in 1972, some afternoons would find a ten-year-old John Koegel mowing the lawn, and a few years after that he was working in the production area. He left for Albion College in 1981 and, after also playing hockey for the college, earned an economics and management degree in 1985, graduating magna cum laude and attaining Albion College Fellow status. He then got into special projects at the family's plant and, after a time, in sales, where he admits to outselling production. He's quoted as saying, "I had about five hundred accounts. I asked my dad [second-generation Albert Koegel] how we could grow sales if we couldn't keep up production." After apparently asking the question one too many times, John Koegel became president of the company in 1994, when his father was only sixty-eight years old.[157]

The transition didn't mean John's dad retired. Albert remained as CEO of the company, continuing to do the bookkeeping on a daily basis well into his eighties and early nineties. He remained active as well, and in 2008 he ran his first Crim ten-mile run using a one-mile-run/one-mile-walk technique at the age of eighty-two with a finish time of 2:52:32.[158] He continued to complete the race intermittently, and in 2012, he finished with a time of 2:52:10, running slightly faster than his first run in 2008. In 2015, at the age of eighty-nine, Albert finished the same run with a time of 3:33:06.[159]

UNIQUE DEVELOPMENTS AND ONE PUBLIC SAUCE RECIPE

In 1984, at their Civic Park Lounge, the Hoenickes registered "Flint's Original Old Greek's Coney Island Recipe" as an officially recognized trademark, complete with a hand-drawn logo. Their sauce was distributed frozen through local retail outlets.[160] The trademark was canceled in 1990, likely due to nonrenewal by the Hoenickes.[161] Due to court action regarding a couple of spaces they'd apparently opened without proper permissions, the Hoenickes subsequently closed the Civic Park Lounge in 2006.[162]

In 1987, Genesee Valley Mall opened a second-floor mezzanine in its center court, relocating some of the restaurants in the mall to a new food court upstairs.[163] Gus and Angelo Vergos's Palace Coney Island was one of the restaurants to make this move.[164]

In 1985, David Gillie opened what is one of the most unique Flint coney restaurants. He built his western-themed restaurant at the corner of Dort Highway and Stanley Roads in Mt. Morris. The restaurant has become so popular Gillie added a second parallel drive-through. The ten-gallon-hat-wearing coin collector accepts most forms of payments, including, as per the restaurant's former website, Euros, norfed Liberty Dollars and "pre-1965 US Silver at twenty times face."[165]

I'd mentioned one of Krueger's attempts at correcting the folklore surrounding Joy Gallagher's ground hot dog recipe that was published in the *Journal* on January 6, 1998. We do need to look at one sentence in this column, that being, "First, no former or current coney island restaurant has ever revealed its sauce recipe."[166] It turns out this wasn't the case.

In 1991, the Michigan Restaurant Association published *A Taste of Michigan*, a collection of more than two hundred recipes from Michigan restaurants, including the venerable Bavarian Inn in Frankenmuth, the Hathaway House in Blissfield and Stafford's Bay View Inn in Petoskey. David Gillie also contributed a recipe to this book, one that deserves a closer look. It is called "Gillie's Flint Coney Island Hot Dog Chili Topping" and involves sautéing diced onions in hot oil; adding some paprika, cumin and chili powder; then adding ground beef to simmer.[167]

Dave explained to me in an email, "I made one change in that published recipe: I changed the normal extra fine raw ground 'beef, beef heart, soy texture' that I buy from Abbott's Meat in 25 lb. bags with suggesting they use lean hamburg and grind it extra fine. (I might have suggested trying to find beef heart?)" While he may have suggested this modification, it did not show up in the final publication.

"However, sometime after that, Abbott's Meat started making four-pound and ten-pound Coney Sauce packs so that homes, bars and small restaurants could also make their own Flint-style coney sauce. I would recommend this now instead of trying to find/get extra-fine ground hamburger."

Gillie did verify to me that the recipe in *A Taste of Michigan* is close to what he makes at Gillie's Coney Island. "The book recipe was slightly modified for publication [from what we make] just to accommodate being done at home." My test of Gillie's recipe from *A Taste of Michigan* is included in the Recipes appendix.

In an email, Gillie also gave his opinion on shops that offer multiple varieties of coneys:

> *It's been getting a bit weird here lately as Detroit Coney Island owners have been moving into the Flint area. Their style of chili is so much different and customers are getting more and more confused about what they are going to get. I'm one of the few hold-outs not offering both styles—I really think Flint should stay special with their own style and I've not an idea how to make theirs anyways. Guess I could buy it, but so far I've placated those Detroiters by using bowl chili as a topping if they insist.*

Meanwhile, during his visits to Flint, basketball player Marty Embry went to Angelo's every weekend to eat. After a while, Angelo Branoff pointedly asked if Embry were interested in buying the restaurant. The 6'9" power center had no knowledge of the restaurant business or any desire to actually open a Coney Island restaurant, and it was out of his price range by at least $1 million anyway.

THE THIRD GENERATION

The third generation of Flint coney ownership began in 1998 with the purchase of Angelo's by a partnership that had Neil Helmkay as president and Tom Zelevarovski as vice president. Zelevarovski had arrived in the United States from Macedonia in 1977, started his restaurant career at U.S. Coney Island and owned New Port Coney Island Family Diner in Owosso with Kosta Panos (owner of numerous Coney Islands, including the Apollo in Davison and Kosta's on Corunna Road) from 1992 to 1997. Tom later moved to work as a cook at Scotti's in Burton and then worked at his cousin's place, Angelo's, for twenty years.[168]

Zef Dedivanaj immigrated to Detroit from Albania in 1965 at the age of sixteen, washing dishes at the venerable Lafayette Coney Island. It's been noted there are more Albanian immigrants in the Detroit area than anywhere else outside Europe. An even larger influx of immigrations after about 1990 occurred because of the collapse of the communist government there and the resulting economic crisis.[169] The Albanians' business of choice in the Detroit area appears to be the Coney Island.[170] Dedivanaj opened his first coney shop in 1984, Motor City Coney Island, then moved his family to Fenton in 1987, subsequently moving his shop in 1994 to Gratiot Avenue with the name Mega Coney Island. The shop closed a few years later.[171]

In 1999, Dedivanaj and sons George and Rocky opened Mega Coney Island in Fenton at the Owen Road exit off I-75. They then also opened the Mega Classic Diner in Flint Township in 2007. The restaurants offer the classic Coney Island menus from the 1970s and '80s, and also serve both Flint- and Detroit-style coneys.[172]

Government "Economic Development" Handouts Rob Peter to Pay Paul by Michael D. LaFaive

Originally published in "Viewpoint on Public Issues," February 7, 2000, No. 2000-08, ISSN 1093-2240, by the Mackinac Center for Public Policy, Midland, Michigan

Last November [1999], when Governor Engler vetoed a bill to exempt certain politically favored groups from a particular tax, he wisely declared, "Tax policy is best which is simple and uniform, and which treats similarly situated activities in the same manner." He was precisely right. It is poor economics and fundamentally unfair for government to pick winners and losers by providing special breaks, favors, or subsidies to certain firms and not their competitors. The only problem is, others within state government are doing exactly that.

Consider the case of Boar's Head Provision Company—a meat products company headquartered in Brooklyn, New York. In exchange for the company's promise to invest $14 million and create 450 new jobs in Michigan over the next three years, the Michigan Jobs Commission arranged in 1998 to give Boar's Head an "economic development package" worth up to $5.1 million in federal, state, and local resources. It includes up to $3 million for equipment leasing, an abatement of the 6-mill state education tax of up to $212,590, and as much as $1,000 per worker for training. Armed with these "incentives," the company opened a processing plant near Holland, Michigan, on December 13, 1999.

The successor agency to the old Michigan Jobs Commission is now known as the Michigan Economic Development Corporation (MEDC). Its highly paid bureaucrats will count 450 "new" jobs as the agency's contribution to the Michigan economy through the Boar's Head deal. What its press releases will not reveal is the impact of the deal on other Michigan businesses, such as Koegel Meats, Inc., in Flint.

Like Boar's Head, Koegel makes meat products. A Michigan-based family business for three generations, it produces an extensive line of cold cuts and the popular "Koegel's Vienna Frankfurters" that get grilled by the millions in Michigan back yards every summer. Its meat products still use recipes devised by Albert Koegel when he emigrated from Germany to Michigan and started the company in 1916. The firm sells 99 percent of its product in Michigan and employs 110 people at its Flint facility.

Al Koegel, son of the founder, is not one to make a big fuss about unfair competition. Like his dad before him and his son John who will carry on after him, Al would rather run the business than spend time lobbying politicians. He cannot help but point out when asked, however, that for all of its 84 years, Koegel Meats always paid its taxes and never took a dime of taxpayer money: no abatements, no subsidies. The company always trained its own employees with its own funds. In fact, when the company was once offered federal money for job training, Al turned it down because he did not want the hassle of red tape and paperwork.

So we have here the classic American Dream story: A German immigrant comes to America seeking opportunity, settles in Michigan, starts a company, works hard, and succeeds. His family keeps the business here through thick and thin in one of the most high-tax, economically distressed areas of the state. They focus on customers, not government, and grow the business—taking no public money and paying full freight in taxes year in and year out. Now along come the wizards at the MEDC who, in the name of "economic development," take money from taxpayers including the Koegel family business and give it to a New York competitor.

There is something seriously wrong with this picture. Lansing bureaucrats, most of whom probably do not know how to run a business, will take credit for their vision and thoughtfulness when they should be scolded for corrupting Michigan's economy. A state agency will claim it "created" 450 jobs without perhaps even a single reporter asking tough questions like, "How many jobs may be lost or may never come into being at other Michigan meat product companies like Koegel in Flint or Kowalski in Hamtramck?" or, "Where will Boar's Head's workers come from in the tightest labor market in 30 years, and who will pay the bill for their previous employers to go out and find replacement workers?"

The Boar's Head handout may be "economic development" in Lansing, but in the real world, it is just another example of robbing Peter to pay Paul.

(Michael D. LaFaive is a policy analyst with the Mackinac Center for Public Policy, a research and educational institute headquartered in Midland, Michigan. More information on economic development is available at www.mackinac.org. Permission to reprint in whole or in part is hereby granted, provided that the author and his affiliation are cited.)

By the year 2000, Marty Embry had retired from professional basketball, moved back to Flint and immediately got into various businesses. He told me, "Flint has always been my safe haven, even though most folks think that it's too dangerous to live there."

But back at Angelo's, something happened between Helmkay and Zelevarovski, a storied conflict that varied depending on the source. In the early 2000s, Zelevarovski left Angelo's. A few loyal employees followed, and in 2003 Zelevarovski established Tom Z's Original Coney Island at the intersection of Court Street and Grand Traverse, just west of downtown Flint.[173]

After Helmkay and Zelevarovski parted ways in 2003, Embry frequented Tom Z's Original Coney Island out of allegiance to him. Because of Embry's love of cooking, Zelevarovski asked if he would be interested in opening another Tom Z's location. Embry agreed, and Zelevarovski began to train him in the nuances of Macedonian coney prep. Zelevarovski and Angelo Branoff taught Embry their recipe with one condition: don't share the recipe with anyone, which Embry has never done.

Embry opened a Tom Z's Original Coney Island in Mt. Morris later in 2003, owning it on his own while using the Tom Z's name and menu, along with Zelevarovski's recipe for Flint coney sauce, while making most of his own menu items from scratch. Once Embry founded the location, Zelevarovski sent a few of his people over until Embry hired and trained his own cashiers. Embry says Zelevarovski made it easy to open a location because he was a walking pillar of information.

MORE RETAIL SALES

Victoria Lynch created Lynch Shipping Services in Harrison, Michigan, in 2004 specifically to partner with Koegel Meats to provide overnight shipping of Koegel's products nationwide. The buykoegels.com website officially offers Koegel's entire product line, including Al Koegel's Coney Franks and the four- and ten-pound bags of frozen and uncooked Abbott's Original Coney Island Topping.[174]

In 2004, Marty Embry came up with a unique concept for a product: a Flint Coney Sauce Spice. The idea was to develop it as a spice blend that could be mixed with various ground meats to create an accurate Flint coney sauce at home. It took about a year or so before he had that aha moment. Once the final missing ingredient was added to the mix (something technically not a "spice" but more of a technique), Embry finally felt ready to take the product to market. He located a company to blend and package the spice mix, taking another three months of testing before he was satisfied with the work. Embry began selling the spice blend on his website in 2005, about the same time that he closed his Mt. Morris Tom Z's location.

DOCUMENTING THE STORY

In 1998, an event was held at the Koegel's plant on Bristol Road. Genesee County Historical Society researchers Bob Florine, Matt Davison and Sally Jaeger had assembled a number of images from the history of the

Flint coney and projected them as a slideshow, along with a description of anecdotes from the heyday of the Flint coney. The researchers then compiled the information, and in 2007 the historical society published the info as the twenty-four-page *Two to Go: A Short History of Flint's Coney Island Restaurants*. There were maps with ownership histories, and on the back page were Joy Gallagher's two sauce recipes circa 1978, the one with ground hot dogs and the other with beef heart and cumin.[175] The publication succeeded in presenting a history of the Flint coney to the public for the first time, including a number of previously unknown details.

THE FLINT CONEY IN THE TWENTY-FIRST CENTURY

ONLINE HOAX RECIPES

As the internet grew, many hoax recipes for the Flint coney sauce were promulgated online. Joy Gallagher's Flint coney recipe containing ground hot dogs[176] gained considerable momentum and was posted on dozens of sites as "the original recipe," with credit given to various families and friends of those posting it or of restaurant owners.

There are others as well. For example, if and when you come across the following supposedly original recipe for Flint coney sauce on the web, please don't try it. The organ taste is quite strong and the aftertaste even stronger. I rarely throw away dishes that I've made, but this one definitely didn't make it and ended up in the trash after one spoonful. This is probably one of those recipes that was posted to the internet before the person who posted it even tried it, even though it was posted as "(tried)":

Flint's Original Coney Sauce Recipe
Ingredients
½ pound of beef kidney
½ pound of beef heart
3 tbsp of paprika
2 tbsp of chili powder
¼ [cup] veg. oil
Salt to taste

Directions

1. Have your butcher grind kidney and heart.

2. Start by mixing all ingredients except oil in an adequately sized sauce pan. Since meat is very dry, slowly add in oil before turning on heat.

3. Mix well over medium heat, and allow to simmer on low heat for about 45 minutes. May need to add in more oil, since you don't want mix to "fry dry."

4. I always use a Vienna warm dog (Koegel's are the best), Coney Sauce, diced onions, and mustard top the bun.

5. Cannot get this in a restaurant except in Flint, MI.

THE ISSUES WITH "SECRET" RECIPES

The recipes for the majority of the Flint coney sauces have been closely guarded secrets for decades. This concept is in line with a lot of thinking in the food industry that direct competition is to be avoided at all costs. Nondisclosure agreements have become standard practice: the Kellogg's plant in Battle Creek, Michigan, ceased real factory tours in 1986 because of certain product advancements, and many home cooks claim secret ingredients in their signature dishes. The concept of secret recipes is parodied in the 2008 animated film *Kung Fu Panda* in Mr. Ping's "secret ingredient soup."

Meanwhile, the Chelsea Milling Company in Chelsea, Michigan, still gives one-hour tours of its one-and-only Jiffy Mix plant, revealing during the tours that the "blueberries" in the muffin mixes are actually colored-and-flavored dried chunks of apple because dried blueberries don't last as long. Margaret Rudkin, the founder of Pepperidge Farm, published a hardbound cookbook in 1963; in one of many such examples, she told the complete story of the brand's Sage & Onion Stuffing, which was the first commercial stuffing mix, complete with her grandmother's original recipe. And countless restaurants, such as eve (all lowercase) in Ann Arbor and Les Halles in New York City and the contributors to the 1991 Michigan Restaurant Association's *A Taste of Michigan* have published individual recipes, or complete collections, directly off their menus, scaled down for the home cook.

The *Les Halles Cookbook*, written by the restaurant's executive chef at-large, the late Anthony Bourdain, is most unique in that the Park Avenue location of Les Halles also sold products directly out of its own butcher shop. This meant home cooks could go to Les Halles; buy the beef, chicken, pork and lamb prepared by the same butchers on-site for the restaurant's own cookline; take those meats and poultry home; and use Bourdain's own recipes from the restaurant to cook the restaurant's dishes themselves. The restaurant closed in March 2016.[177]

BUSINESS DECISIONS

The scrap collector who collected Simion Brayan's Flint's Original sign in 1980 contacted Tom Zelevarovski in late 2007 about the sign, which the scrapper had been keeping in his garage. Tom Z's had been partly destroyed by a fire on September 10, 2007,[178] and was undergoing a $400,000 restoration. Zelevarovski subsequently reopened the restaurant in 2008 as Flint's Original Coney Island, with Brayan's restored sign out front.[179]

The year 2008 saw the opening of another of one of the most unique hot dog stands ever put together. Chris and Jeremy Gocha founded Lake Dogs on Lobdell Lake in southwest Genesee County near Fenton. Not *near* the lake—*on* it. Lake Dogs was a Flint coney shop built on the deck of a pontoon boat. Service was either at one of the docks, at the Lake Dogs vessel as a boat pulled up to it, or the Lake Dogs vessel would travel to a requested location.[180]

By 2009, Facebook had become rather ubiquitous. Jenn Barber grew up eating Flint coneys at Angelo's, but in 2009, she was working in San Diego as a social media strategist. At one point, she traveled to Flint by way of Detroit Metro Airport, returned to the Detroit area and realized she hadn't eaten a single Flint coney. She found a Detroit coney shop, ordered one and completely disliked it. That evening, she started the Flint-Style Coney Dog Facebook page. By late 2020, Barber's page had more than 2,700 likes.[181]

AC Spark Plug, whose workers had helped make Angelo's so popular, underwent a number of changes over the decades and became part of Delphi when that group was formed in 1995. Delphi declared bankruptcy only a decade later in 2005. Employment numbers at the massive complex near Angelo's peaked at around 14,000, but by 2007 only 1,100 hourly workers were there. Production ceased in 2007, and by 2017 the property had been sold.[182]

I met Marty Embry on Facebook in 2010 and discovered he and I are, as Marty puts it, "fellow coneyheads." I prepared a sauce as per Marty's recipe with his Coney Sauce Spice and found that it was extremely close to some of my favorite Flint coney sauces. Marty also opened the southern restaurant

51 to Go on Clio Road at Carpenter in 2014, offering authentic southern cooking to Flint diners until they "have dined sufficiently." And while he still offered his Flint Coney Spice and other unique spice blends, there were no coneys on the menu at 51 to Go.

In late 2014, Marty Embry told me, "I have met some of the most interesting people because of my love of cooking. Coneys and Coney Joints are a working man's restaurant. That's where you go to meet old friends, make new friends, the waitresses know your name as well as your kids, the owners are visible and the food is cheap and good! Even though I now own a Southern themed restaurant, I still wanted to keep that same ideology based on the coney joints." In January 2015, Embry's Flint Coney Sauce Spice, as well as his own seasoning spice blend, were available at Shorthorn Meats in Mt. Morris, the first grocery to give his spices shelf space.[183] But Embry closed the restaurant in late 2015, also discontinuing his Coney Sauce Spice, all for personal health reasons. Fortunately, though, he began offering the spice again in mid-2020 from his home in Morrisville, North Carolina.

On December 29, 2010, Terry Thomas sold the venerable Flint-based family-owned Halo Burger to Dortch Enterprises, a Subway franchisee with more than sixty restaurants. Thomas had inherited the company from his father, William V. Thomas, who started as a Kewpee operator back in the 1930s and went private with his Halo Burger brand in 1967. Terry Thomas's sons weren't interested in the business, hence the sale to Dortch Enterprises.

Meatpacker Otto W. Liebold had been in operation in downtown Flint since 1968 and provided the fresh-ground meat to Halo Burger for its quarter- and half-pound burgers. Liebold was purchased by Evans Foodservice of

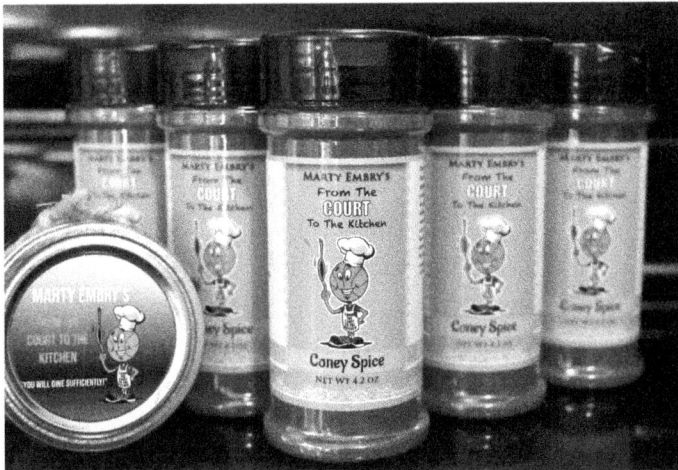

Five jars of Marty Embry's coney spice, along with one of his handmade Kentucky bourbon–scented soy candles. *Author collection.*

Swartz Creek in 2005.[184] At some point, Halo Burger began purchasing meat from Abbott's, and by 2019, the chain had added the Flint coney to the menus of its restaurants. Halo Burger also offered beer in at least one of its locations.[185]

One of the more interesting aspects of the Halo Burger menu addition at that time was that it included nutritional information that, by law, had been collected through physical tests of the product. As Halo Burger gets the ground beef for its burgers from Abbott's Meat, we can assume their Flint coney is made up of the Koegel Coney Frank and Abbott's Coney Topping. Combining the info gives the following complete information:

Flint Coney Nutrition Information
Ingredients: Koegel's Coney Franks (Beef, Pork, Water, Salt, Spices, Sugar, Sodium Citrate, Dextrose, Sodium Diacetate, Nonfat Dry Milk, Sodium Erythorbate, Spice Extractives, Sodium Nitrite, Garlic, stuffed into lamb casing)

Abbott's Coney Topping (Beef Hearts, Beef, Water, Textured Vegetable Protein (Soy Flour, Caramel Color), Onions, Spices, Salt, Monosodium Glutamate, Sodium Nitrate, Garlic Powder, Sodium Erythorbate, Dextrose, Sugar, and Sodium Nitrite)

Serving Size (g)	169
Calories	411
Calories from Fat	216
Total Fat (g)	23
Saturated Fat (g)	8
Trans Fat (g)	0

CONTAINS: Dairy, Wheat, Gluten, Soy

Cholesterol (mg)	56
Sodium (mg)	1000
Carbohydrates (g)	33
Fiber (g)	1
Sugars (g)	6
Protein (g)	14

Because of where this information was located, it is now included in a number of nutrition-tracking applications for both computer and cellphone use.

The year 2011 saw the beginning of what may have been considerable growth for Angelo's as it opened a second location on Dort Highway at Bristol Road. In 2012, a third location opened on Grand Blanc Road at US-23, along with a fourth location in Mt. Morris in 2013. In 2012, Neil Helmkay said he felt there was room for twelve to fifteen Angelo's in Genesee County alone.[186]

Also in 2011, City of Davison's Mayor Pro Tem Tim Bishop was elected mayor of that city, and at the 2012 Fat Tuesday celebration, he won the Paczki Eating Contest. He had owned and operated the Locker Room, a sporting goods store, but then closed it in 2012 to begin operation of B-Dogs Specialty Hot Dog Cart within the city for street-side operation, at public events and at various festivals and events. Referring to it as his "mobile office," Bishop entertained conversations from residents who wanted to discuss city business with him while enjoying his various styles of hot dogs and coneys.[187]

In 2015, Bishop also began operating his cart at the newer Flint Farmer's Market, where B-Dog's menu included the Stadium Dog (ketchup, mustard, onions and relish), the Backyard BBQ (bacon, onions, BBQ sauce and a pickle slice), the Dirty South (Flint-style coney topping, coleslaw, mustard and onions), the Mac Daddy (mac 'n' cheese, bacon and onions), the Deep South (coleslaw, mustard and onions), Flint's Original Coney (Flint-style coney topping, mustard and onions), the Big Pig (Flint-style coney topping, bacon, mustard and onions), the BLT Dog (bacon, lettuce, tomato and mayonnaise) and the Coney Crunch (Flint-style coney topping, melted cheese, crushed Fritos and jalapeños). Bishop is still actively operating B-Dog's at the time of this writing in late 2021.

Scotti's Coney Island had been in operation at Belsay and Lapeer Roads in Burton since opening in 1970 by John Bibilikow and James Brown. It was then operated by Stavros Kuzmanovsky and Russell Hinton until Hinton left in 2000. Marino and Christina Matsoukis purchased the restaurant in early 2008 and reopened it as Romey's, with instructions not to change the fish and chips recipe.[188] The restaurant then again became available for purchase in 2010. Atanas "Tom" Zelevarovski of Tom Z's, who had previously been employed at the restaurant beginning in 1977, purchased Romey's, gave it a complete remodel and renamed it as Scotti's once again, serving the same unchanged fish and chips recipe alongside his Flint coneys.[189] By early 2011,

Scotti's was reopened under the same name and finally a 24/7 operation.[190] At some point along the way, Zelevarovski closed his original Tom Z's Court Street location.

In 2014, Chris and Jeremy Gocha posted on their website that they were selling the pontoon boat–based Lake Dogs business on Lobdell Lake near Fenton. By the end of the year, their website had gone dark.

In December 2014, a For Sale sign appeared in front of the original Angelo's location on Davison Road. Owner Neil Helmkay said he wanted to explore other opportunities and that he planned to "include in the contract that the recipes for food remain the same."[191] The Angelo's expansion locations in Mt. Morris and on Dort Highway then closed in 2015.

In May 2015, apparently there was an issue with the casings of Koegel's Viennas becoming quite hard when cooked. Complaints appeared on Koegel's Facebook page, and John Koegel himself provided the explanation by describing a few basic concepts of meatpacking:

> *Thank you for your post inquiring about our casings. Please accept my apology for these incidents. Natural casings vary in tenderness based on the country of origin, age and diet of the sheep. We usually get the best selection because we are one of the largest producers of natural casing products in the Midwest. We try to make sure that we stuff the casing fully without breaking them and steam them properly, steaming tenderizes a natural casing. Unfortunately, we do not know a casing is tough until it is being eaten and by that time we are into a new lot. We have not changed anything but it is a variable we cannot always control. Again, thank you for your post. Sincerely, John Koegel*

While Koegel wrote "sheep," remember that a lamb is a young sheep. Both the Vienna and the coney use lamb casings versus the sheep casing on many hot dogs used for Detroit-style coney dogs, which is why those products seem to be more chewy than their Flint counterparts.

On December 16, 2015, WJRT reported Koegel's was donating $35,000 to the Flint Community Schools in support of the schools' band programs. The project was in partnership with an instrument refurbishment program called the Green Horn Project, which provided lower-cost rebuilt instruments to school programs for band students to freely use.

THE GOTHIC FUNK-STYLE CONEY

Many books about different styles of hot dogs and coneys have represented the Flint coney with varying degrees of accuracy. The majority follow the folklore and incorrectly include a version of, or a reference to, Joy Gallagher's sauce recipe containing ground hot dogs, saying it's the original recipe. Oddly enough, *Coney Detroit* by Katherine Yung and Joe Grimm gives one of the more accurate representations of the Flint coney, while offering no recipe. The authors also wrote of the Jackson coney, showing a fairness unseen in many Detroit coney aficionados.[192]

In May 2015, Connor Coyle published his book *Atlas: Short Stories* at his own Gothic Funk Press. In 2010, Coyle founded the publishing company in Chicago and moved it to Flint in 2012, when he relocated back to his hometown. The collection seems to have had too quiet a release. Written in a Gothic Funk style, with a cover photo of the sign at Atlas Coney Island, the Flint-centric short stories are laced with interesting information and real history about the Flint coney. What's interesting about the book is the accuracy about the history and makeup of the Flint coney as told in the Gothic Funk style. Koegel's becomes the "Richard Goerlich Bavarian Encased Meat Company, later known simply as 'Goerlich's'" (just as Koegel Meats Inc. is simply referred to as "Koegel's"), autoworkers are referred to as "Automobilians" and Flint itself is "Akawe," the author's fictionalized city referred to in other works. But the accuracy within the fictionalized narrative is spot-on, with this description of the sauce: "Finely ground beef heart and beef kidney, mixed with beef suet, browned minced onions, and sanguined spices...something magical. Nobody knows what but the coney chefs, and if they told then they would not be gods."[193]

THE 2014 FLINT WATER CRISIS

Switching away from the city of Detroit as a source, the city of Flint once again began pulling water for its residents from the Flint River in April 2014. It wasn't too long afterward the city's water tested positive for an excess of total trihalomethanes, which is a disinfection byproduct. With concerns about Flint's water quality drawing national attention and long-term solutions not yet fully developed, David Gillie began offering free well water to Flint residents, drawn from a 350-foot depth into the Great Lakes Aquifer via the two spigots at Gillie's Coney Island in January 2015.[194]

But Flint's water system was in considerably worse shape than was originally thought. Between January and June 2015, water tested at residences in Flint showed escalating lead levels. In the fall, attention escalated further at the national level, with multiple media and network broadcasters reporting on the crisis. On January 19, 2016, Koegel Meats issued the following statement:

> *Koegel Meats is NOT Connected to the City of Flint Water System. We wish to assure our customers that the processing of Koegel Meat products has not been affected by the City of Flint water crisis. We are concerned like so many others about the current water issues facing the City of Flint and its residents. Koegel's purchases its water from Flint Township and the Township acquires the water from a totally separate system not affected by the issues the City of Flint is experiencing. In addition, we further filter water to a higher degree before using it in our recipes. On behalf of the Koegel Family and our employees—thank you for choosing Koegel's!*

Similarly, Abbott's Meat posted its own test data both on the company's Facebook page and on the receptionist's window where customers would walk in to purchase products at the plant.

Tom Z had this to say to *Eater Detroit* about the water crisis: "People don't want to eat. The first question is: Do you got city water? Yes. Then you got filters? Yes. It doesn't do any good....It used to be auto city; now it's poison city." He had installed multiple water filters within Tom Z's but told *Eater* business was so slow he was actually considering closing down.[195]

On January 21, 2016, the *New York Times* published a detailed timeline of events surrounding the crisis up to that date.[196] With such organizations focusing on Flint, CNN hosted a Democratic presidential debate at The Whiting on March 6, 2016, two days prior to the Michigan Primary. Davison's Mayor Tim Bishop served his specialties from his B-Dog's cart, including his Flint's Original Coney, inside CNN's "Spin Room" at the University of Michigan–Flint recreation center.

On the day of the 2016 Michigan Primary, NPR broadcast a piece titled "Tests Say the Water Is Safe. But Flint's Restaurants Still Struggle." In the online version of the piece, a photo showed a sign on the door of the Westside Diner that stated, "We DO NOT use Flint water!! We use Detroit water. If in doubt, you may verify this information with the Flint Township Water Department." Another image showed Angelo's Coney Island manager Carlos Amos in front of a stack of bottled water, talking with Anthony

Pavone, supervisor of the Genesee County Health Department. The piece included the following about Angelo's:

> *A sign at the front of the restaurant says: "All of our beverages and ice are made with filtered water." But even here, says manager Carlos Amos, business is down. "The first question out of everybody's mouth is, 'Do you have Flint water?'"…Amos says the restaurant's owner bought a new filtration system and stacks of bottled water to sell to customers who prefer it. On every table, there's a copy of an inspection report showing no lead in Coney Island's water….Mason Miller, a General Motors retiree eating breakfast at the restaurant, says he doesn't pay much attention to the signs, because he expects clean water. "You would think that would be the No. 1 priority on a restaurant list—to make sure that people could come in here and be safe," he says.*[197]

As events unfolded, the Flint coney businesses continued to be the center of attention for reports about the water crisis. In a piece on March 30, 2016, *Flint Journal* journalist Robert Acosta reported that Huntington Bank and the FlintNow Foundation, founded by Detroit Pistons owner Tom Gores, had put together a $25 million program to help businesses affected by the water crisis. Similar programs had been put together in seventeen other Michigan counties since 2013, and many businesses had already taken microloans from the other programs. Atlas Coney Island on Corunna Road was mentioned throughout the piece as an example of what businesses were seeing as a result of the crisis. John Todorovsky, third-generation owner of the Atlas, was quoted as saying, "Ninety percent of our customers, they have the perception that the water is tainted….We're not a dry cleaner or selling shoes or tires. We're selling food and drink….Anything to help us say we are open for business, Flint is open for business, is welcome."[198]

On June 16, 2016, it was announced that thirty businesses affected by the Flint water crisis would share in $269,500 in grants from the Moving Flint Forward Fund, with awards ranging from $5,000 to $10,000. Angelo's Coney Island was included in the list for funds to go toward "new equipment, repairs, inventory, working capital, water filtration systems and reimbursements, vendor payments and marketing or advertising needs." The awards came from the $25 million fund provided by Huntington Bank and the FlintNow Foundation, through the Flint and Genesee County Chamber of Commerce.[199]

2016 AND KOEGEL MEATS' ONE-HUNDREDTH ANNIVERSARY

By early 2016, Halo Burger was back down to fifteen locations when Dortch Enterprises sold it to an investment firm called Halo Country LLC, with oil and gas entrepreneur and investment banker Chance Richie as CEO and majority owner.[200] One of Richie's first efforts was to put together a Halo Burger food truck for future use at events, festivals and meetings.[201]

Overshadowed by the Flint water crisis, Koegel Meats celebrated its one-hundredth anniversary in 2016 with numerous media reports. On January 1, the company posted the following on its Facebook page:

> *Thank you to EVERYONE who helped our family reach a major benchmark for Koegel's…our 100th Anniversary! It was 100 years ago that Albert Koegel came to the Flint area following his training in an apprenticeship program in Germany in 1916. Today we still use his unique recipes to create our signature flavors and products. Thank you to the many generations that have made our family recipes part of your family traditions. Happy New Year!*

In a one-hundredth anniversary report on February 10, WJRT quoted John Koegel as saying in 2015 the company "shipped out close to 12,000,000 hot dogs.…'That's a lot and I'd love to do a lot more. It's not too insane, and again, we're a small player. That doesn't include our skinless franks, our skinless polish or something like that,' Koegel said."[202] The following day, Mlive listed five things to know about Koegel's. Two of the items were that damp sawdust is used for smoking the meats and that the brick floor of the production area is there because of an acid in meat that would cause a concrete floor to erode.[203]

THE GRILL BENZIE FOOD TRUCK

In May 2016, the Goodwill Fresh Start program in Benzie County, on the Lake Michigan shoreline east of Traverse City, including Sleeping Bear Sand Dunes, decided it would not be operating a food truck. The program then leased the vehicle to Grow Benzie, a farmstead community located in an abandoned farm in Benzonia, Michigan. The facilities at the farmstead include a farmer's market, community garden plots, a sewing studio, hoop house–style greenhouses for community use and an incubator kitchen for use by residents wanting to take advantage of Michigan's Cottage Food Laws.[204]

The Grill Benzie food truck made its debut at a Benzie County Chamber of Commerce's Business After Hours event. Grill Benzie then began to be open at Grow Benzie's own Festival Farmer's Market on June 6, 2016, with plans to be open each Monday for the entire season and at the Elberta Farmer's Market on Thursdays as well for breakfast. The southwestern-style menu for the truck rotated, featuring other dishes such as "cream of asparagus soup, tuna salad and tomato mozzarella salad, both with pesto, using the Grow Benzie garden's greens, asparagus, basil, garlic and 42 tomato varieties." The menu also included Michigan-specific dishes such as pasties and both the Detroit- and Flint-style coneys.[205]

THE FLINT CONEY OUTSIDE GENESEE COUNTY

In his 2012 book *Man Bites Dog: Hot Dog Culture in America*, author Bruce Kraig mentioned Tom Z's as one of the top ten places to get an "unusual" hot dog in the United States.[206] June 2012 also saw Angelo's and the Flint coney featured in the in-flight magazine for AirTrans Airlines. The article, titled "Dog & Coney Show," briefly described both the Macedonian cultures and short histories of the coney itself and the restaurant. AirTrans Airlines was subsequently absorbed by Southwest Airlines in 2014, and the article was archived.

A production company from the cable channel TLC descended on the Starlite Coney Island over four nights in late 2012. The network was shooting a pilot for a possible reality show covering the lives of third-shift workers, and the 24/7 Coney Island restaurant provided both a solid location and plenty of non–AC-Delco/Delphi third shifters. While the show wasn't produced, the restaurant and the Flint coney both received good publicity.[207]

By 2012, the Flint coney was being served on regular menus in restaurants such as Sig's Classic Coney Island, which was opened in 2008 as a hot dog cart in Martinsburg, West Virginia.[208] In 2012, the former Longnecks Restaurant at the Kalahari Resort in Sandusky, Ohio, offered the Three Dog Night, which included a Flint-style coney.[209] Just south of Toledo, Swig Restaurant & Bar in Perrysburg, Ohio, opened in 2013 as a charcuterie restaurant. Its handmade and cured coney frank was an accidental re-creation of the Flint coney, which they apparently had never heard of.[210] And in July 2013, the Cape Coral Cruising Club in Cape Coral, Florida, hosted a Flint coney dinner that "consisted of Flint style Coney Island hot dogs, Angelo's special Coney sauce, finely chopped onions and mustard, with steamed buns, potato salad, and Key lime pie."[211]

Beginning in the 2014–15 school year, the Flint coney was being rotated through menus at both the Holmes and Hubbard Dining Halls at Michigan State University in East Lansing. For the 2015–16 school year, the Akers and Brody Dining Halls joined the Holmes Dining Hall in offering the Flint coney.[212]

The year 2014 saw some good publicity for the Flint meat industry and the Flint coney. Angelo's and the Flint coney were listed in "The 24 Best 24-Hour Diners in the U.S." on thrillist.com. The list also included the Fleetwood Diner in Ann Arbor and the Original Pantry Café in Los Angeles.[213] Koegel president (and grandson of Albert Koegel) John C. Koegel gave a complete tour of the Koegel facility to Cheryl Dennison and photographer Mike Naddeo of *MyCity Mag*. Dennison noted that, on that day alone, the facility produced "180,000 skinless beef hot dogs, 160,000 Vienna hot dogs and 20,000 Coney dogs…to name just a few."[214] Note the differentiation between the retail Vienna and the coney used by restaurants in that quote.

On January 15, 2015, in interviewing popular actor and Flint native Terry Crews, then–*Flint Journal* reporter William E. Ketchum III asked Crews which Flint Coney Island he grew up on: "Palace Coney Island. We used to go to Genesee Valley, then go to Palace. I don't remember any shopping trip, ever, not ending with them putting the meat on the dog, the onions and the mustard on those Koegel's. I still have a hankering for those sometimes, man. I can't get it out here in California, when I get back home, that's where I'm headed."[215]

In March 2015, Phil Lopez and Bernice Baldwin were serving Flint-style coneys at Joker Marchant Stadium during the fiftieth Detroit Tigers' Training Camp in Lakeland, Florida. In an article and related video on Major League Baseball's website, MLB journalist Michael Clair wrote of the Flint coney, "Piled high with delicate care by Mr. Lopez, this was a bounty— nay a kaleidoscope of flavors. This hot dog was so good, I forgot to get a picture of it before I started eating. I regret nothing."[216] For the 2017 Detroit Tigers' Training Camp, Detroit Coney Island Co., a coney restaurant in Clearwater Beach, Florida, owned by Dearborn native Dante Guarascio, offered both Flint- and Detroit-style coneys.[217] Flint coneys were on the menu in Lakeland in 2019 as well.[218]

"KOEGEL'S ON THE ROAD"

In early 2015, Victoria Lynch of Lynch Shipping and BuyKoegels.com realized a lot of Flint expatriates and seniors had relocated to certain parts of the country outside the distribution area for Koegel products. She assembled what she called "Koegel's on the Road." Travel dates were announced indicating when Lynch Shipping would bring preordered products to given cities. The 2015 tour began on in late May in Charlotte, North Carolina, continuing in late June in Wichita, Kansas, and then in Lakewood and Colorado Springs. They headed to Tennessee in September, hitting Nashville and Chattanooga; then it was over to Atlanta, Georgia. Thanksgiving week found them in Florida with a busy schedule of Ocala, Zephyrhills, off for Thanksgiving, then Bradenton, Auburndale, and finishing up at Daytona Beach. They completed the year back in Colorado at Loveland and Lakewood on Monday and Tuesday.

The 2016 tour focused more on the West, with Henderson, Nevada, being treated in early January, then Chandler and Tucson, Arizona, the following weekend. It was then back to Henderson, Nevada, in May, then Colorado again for Memorial Day, with visits in Colorado Springs, Aurora and Loveland. Tours continued until the COVID-19 shutdowns in 2020 and resumed again in 2021.

THE RETURN OF FELTMAN'S

In 2015, a pair of Brooklyn natives, brothers Joe and Michael Quinn, revived the circa-1867 Feltman's of Coney Island brand, in honor of their brother Jimmy, who was killed on 9/11. Five years after the reboot, the hot dogs and mustard were available in more than two thousand Whole Foods Markets and Publix groceries nationwide.[219]

A package of the current version of Feltman's of Coney Island's natural casing hot dogs, along with their repackaged mustard. *Author collection.*

LONGEVITY IN THE FLINT CONEY FAMILIES

A clear example of the longevity of Flint coney families was evident for decades at Atlas Coney Island on Corunna Road. Brothers David and Jimmy Todorovsky, born a year apart in Greece in 1933 and 1934, respectively, escaped with their family to Macedonia during World War II, then immigrated to Flint in 1954. Their father owned and operated a series of Flint coney restaurants, including Central Luncheon in 1955, Ritz Drive Inn in 1959 and the Ritz Lounge & Steak House in 1967. The brothers then purchased Atlas Coney Island in 1980. They worked there on alternating twelve-hour shifts every day for thirty-seven years until their retirement on March 22, 2017, at ages eighty-four and eighty-three.

David's daughter Anastasia Pirkovic explained, "The coney was designed for these people at General Motors....They worked so many hours at the plant because production was seven days a week and there was no time to eat....The coney was designed to be hot, nutritious and filling. That's how the coney came about....We are the original. I don't care what anybody says. It started here with the Macedonians way back."[220]

After the brothers' retirement, Atlas Coney Island then closed in 2017. Dominic Berishaj, co-owner of Capt. Coty's with his father, bought the restaurant in 2018 and reopened it as Dom's Diner, which still serves the Flint coney.[221]

THE CLOSING OF THE ORIGINAL ANGELO'S AND LATER DEVELOPMENTS

In November 2017, after more than three years since his first listing Angelo's Coney Island as being for sale, it was reported that Neil Helmkay placed the original Davison Road location under a lease-to-own option to Tim and Paula Stanek, owners of the nearby Chilly's Bar. Unfortunately, on December 28, 2018, Tim Stanek confirmed to the *Flint Journal* that the location had closed during the previous week.

Calling the closing "a sad day for tradition," Stanek stated, "It's sad what's happening to the east side. It's getting worse. It's not getting better. If something doesn't happen soon, we certainly won't be the last [business to close] over there." As the Grand Blanc Road Angelo's location in Mundy Township was still open with MaryAnn Savage as owner, it wasn't the complete demise of the operation.[222]

Shortly after its one-hundredth anniversary celebration on June 26, 2021, Red Hots Coney Island in Highland Park, Michigan—mentioned earlier in the discussion of how Coney Islands were named—closed for good. Unrelated to the COVID-19 pandemic, owner Rich Harlan and his wife, Carol, decided to retire after fifty-five years of making one hundred pounds of their sauce each week. They and their daughter Christina Coden said they still planned to offer tubs of their signature chili in retail stores.[223]

On July 27, 2021, I made the rounds of a few Flint coney shops. At his place in Mt. Morris, Dave Gillie told me he was selling the restaurant to his employees, loaning them the funds from the restaurant against proceeds from future sales. The transaction was completed on October 20, 2021.[224]

And in a conversation with Tom Z at his Scotti's Coney Island in Burton, he let me know he'd sold Simion Brayan's "Flint Original Coney Island Lunch" sign to a collector in Flushing. Its current publicly known whereabouts are unclear.

MAPS

FLINT CONEY HISTORICAL LOCATIONS

FLINT "ORIGINAL" CONEY ISLAND LUNCH

1 FLINT CONEY ISLAND
First Flint Coney Restaurant
202 S. Saginaw St.
1925-1979
George Brown, Owner
Simion P. Brayan, Originator
Paul Branoff, Partner
Steve George, Partner
1927-1929
George Pappadakis, Partner
1980 Demolished

2 200 S. Saginaw St.
1927 - 1929
George Pappadakis Restaurant
1930 - 1941
New System Coney Island Restaurant
1942 - 1945
Chicago Hat Cleaners and Shoe Shine
1946
Hot Puppy Coney Island Restaurant
1947 - 1952
U.S. Coney Island Restaurant no. 2
Bill Stevens
Mike Stablinski
Bill Angeletsey
1954 - 1964
Mike's Coney Island Restaurant
1965 - 1966
Nick's Coney Island Restaurant
1967 - 1971
Mike's Coney Island Restaurant
1972 Vacant
1980 Demolished

3 204 S. Saginaw St.
1916
Le Unas, John Restaurant
1917 - 1921
Home Restaurant
1923
Buick Outfitters Clothing
1924 - 1926
Lincoln Lunch
1927 - 1928
James Trahos Restaurant
1929 - 1930
Light House Lunch
1931 Vacant
1932 - 1936
Allen's Menswear
1937
Flint Shoe Shine
1930
Stanios Restaurant
1940 - 1979
Mad Hatter Shoe Shine
and Hat Blocking
1980 Demolished

4 109 S. Saginaw St.
1927 - 1930
Anthony Nicoloff Restaurant
1931 - 1945
San Juan Chili Parlor
Anthony Nicoloff, Owner
1947 - 1949
Mary Lou Sandwich Shop
1950 - 1953
Miles Grill Restaurant
1954
Nick's Grill Restaurant
1955 - 1959
Tom's Lunch Restaurant
1961 Vacant

5 201 S. Saginaw St.
1935 - 1957
Tasty Coney Island Restaurant
Gus and Harry Yeotis
George Poulos
1958
George N. Brown Coney Island
George Poulos
1959 - 1965
Tasty Coney Island Restaurant
George Poulos
1966 Vacant

6 104 S. Saginaw St.
US. Coney Island Restaurant no. 1
1936 - 1971
Bill Stevens
Mike Stablinski
Bill Angeletsey

7 1901 N. Dort Hwy.
Nite Owl Coney Island
1936 - 1996
Kosta Chokreff
Jim Marx
Chris Christoff
Phill Branott
Simeon Panott
Kosta Panos
Kosta Tragachett
1996 Demolished

8 108 S. Saginaw St.
Famous Coney Island Restaurant
1939 - 1973
George Poulos

9 3306 Corunna Rd.
West Side Coney Island
1947 - 1988
Ralph and Judy Dimond

10 1816 Davison Rd.
Post Office Coney Island
1945 - 1949
John Nichols
Angelo's Coney Island
1949 - 1998
Angelo Nicoloff
Carl Paul
Angelo Popoff
Tom W. Branoff
Tom V. Branoff
Angelo Branoff
1998 - 2003
Neil Helmkay
Tom Zelvrovski
2003 - 2018
Neil Helmkay

11 3600 Dort Hwy.
Star Brothers Coney Island
1987 - 2020
Andy Stergiopoulos
John Stergiopoulos

12 401 W. Court St.
2003 - 2008
Tom Z's Original Coney Island
Tom Zelvrovski
2008 - 2015
Tom Z's Flint's Original
(using the restored blue sign
from 202 S. Saginaw St.)

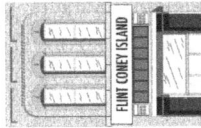

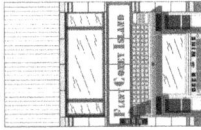

202 S. Saginaw St.
1925 to 1940s
1940s to 1979

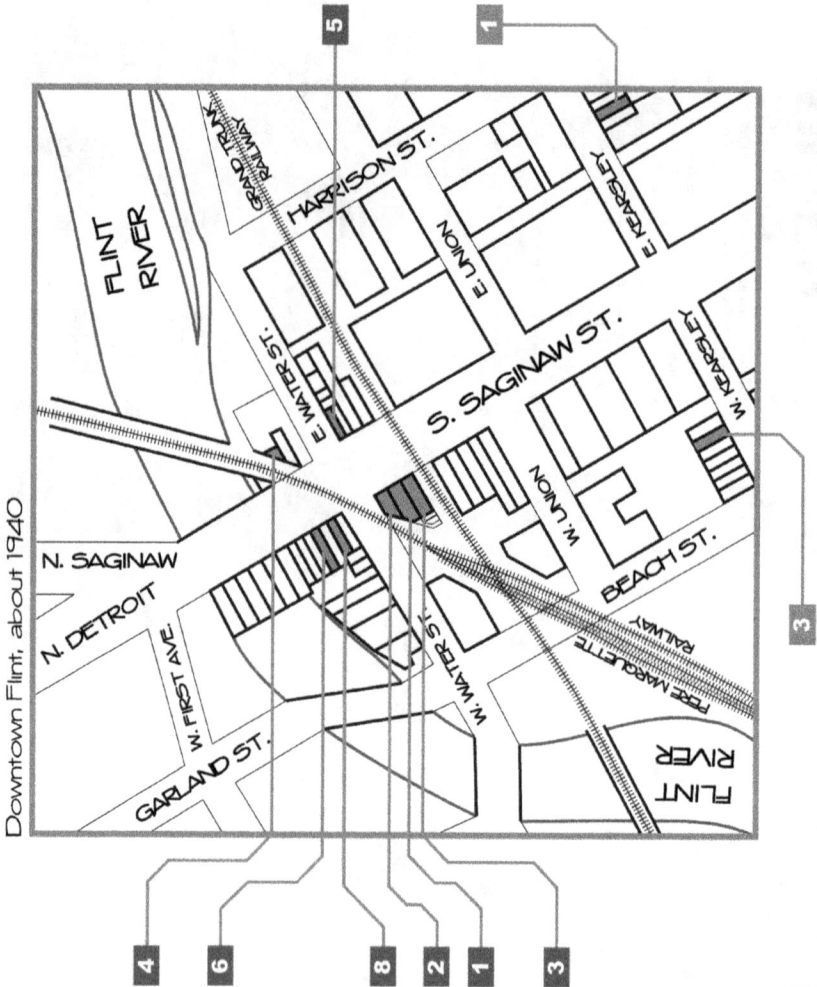

Downtown Flint area map, about 1940. *Author collection.*

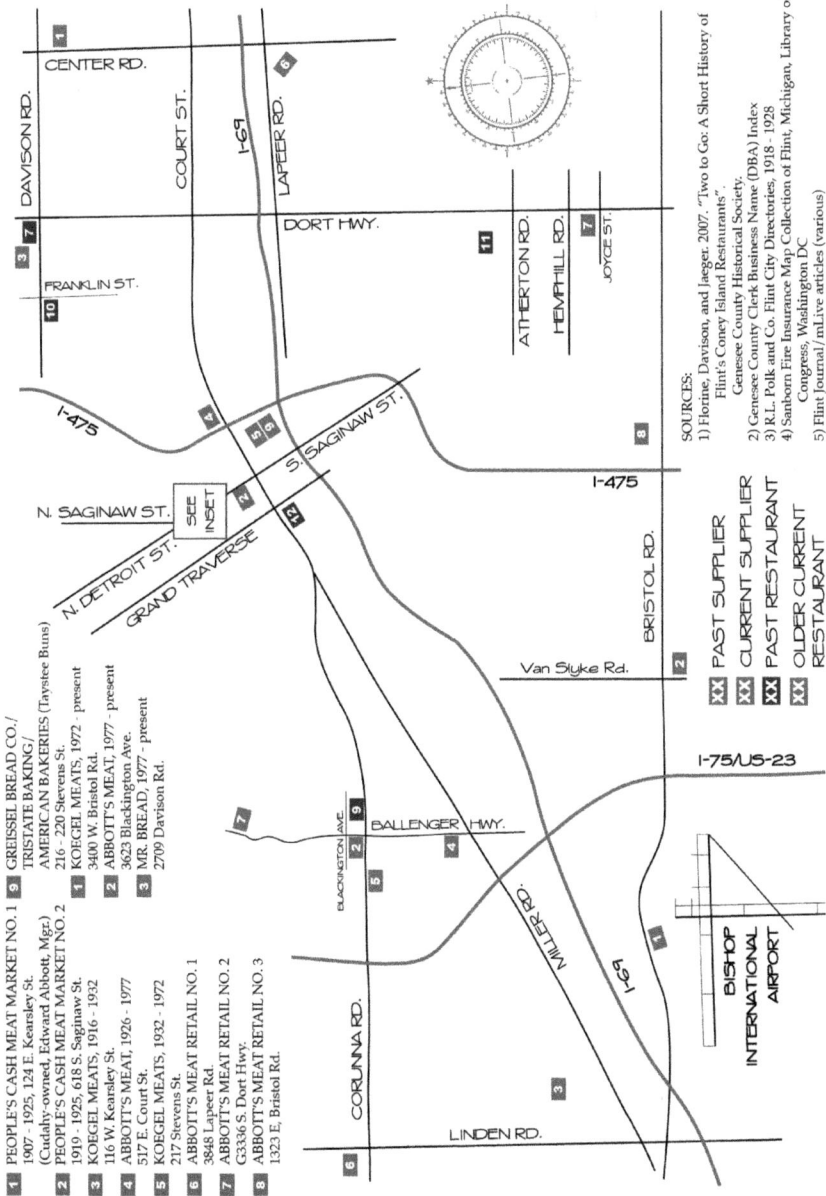

Genesee County current map and location key. *Author collection.*

CONCLUSIONS

*T*he common originating location and culture for the Flint coney was Boufi, Florina, Macedonia, now known as Akritas. Simion P. Brayan, the "father" of the Flint coney and the beginning of the first generation of owners, was from Boufi, as was Vangel T. Nicoloff, the original "Angelo" of Angelo's Coney Island, who can be considered the father of the second generation of owners. The unique flavor and texture of the Flint coney can be traced back to the style of cooking in Boufi in the late 1800s and early 1900s.

The Greek Coney Island restaurant, which also encompasses those begun by families of Macedonian and Albanian cultures, is a uniquely American phenomenon. The mass immigration of people to the United States escaping the horrors of the Balkan Wars of 1903 and 1913 moved them past or through the Coney Island resort at New York City. The Coney Island "style" of hot dog stirred their imagination as a simple but possibly successful method for bringing the warmth and camaraderie of the kafenion from their homeland to their new situation. This included the Nickolson family, who were Greek immigrants and the founders of the Red Hots Coney Island in 1921 in Highland Park, Michigan. Others, such as Macedonian Simion Brayan, would find the Coney Island style existing away from the resort, in the "coney" he ate in Rochester, New York. Brayan's imagination followed similar developments, and he founded his Flint Original near the Flint River in 1925.

It's clear that the acts of the Macedonian and Greek immigrants took to develop their Coney Island restaurants had little to do with money, except for that needed to survive. They brought their families over after settling in a location and developed businesses and long-term employment for their large extended families, establishing simple places where like-minded people could meet in a community space in the familiar style of the kafenion, building a business they could pass down to other family members and creating ethnic communities alongside similarly displaced immigrants where they'd put down new roots.

They succeeded because both the products and sense of family were solid. The immigrants ended up being more financially successful than they could have imagined.

The "Coney Island hot dog" came from the combination of centuries-old German butchering practices that resulted in the development of the frankfurter, which was then topped with a sauce of Greek or Macedonian origin.

Diners tend to be fiercely loyal to not only a particular style of Coney Island hot dog, but many are also just as loyal to a given shop within that style. They like what they grew up with, a particular flavor and texture of a specific coney dog, a given culture and atmosphere of a specific restaurant, owner or server. This can be seen in the coney wars in Detroit, with American and Lafayette Coney Islands being physically side by side. In Flint, this is also seen, given that each restaurant has its own recipe for the ground beef heart base from Abbott's Meat. No one Coney Island Hot Dog or restaurant is "best" and never will be. It's always a matter of personal taste, in the same way as one person liking Jonathan apples more than another who always prefers Granny Smith apples. All arguments in this aside, they're all good in their own way.

It's unclear whether Fort Wayne's Famous Coney Island, Todoroff's Original Coney Island or Virginia Coney Island were the first to open, as specific opening dates in 1914 for those restaurants are unknown. It's also unknown if others opened prior to those two. Accurate information in this regard may never be discovered.

The usage of beef heart is what sets all three coney styles in Michigan apart from other coney styles around the country.

The proud and successful Macedonian and Greek immigrants in Flint wouldn't have ever considered selling to corporate or franchise operations. They would have lost control of their product, they would have had to give up their kafenion and they would have sold off their sense of family pride and community. The people of Boufi, Florina, Macedonia, the Brayans, Branoffs and Nikoloffs, simply weren't raised that way.

CONCLUSIONS

The popularity of the Flint coney and the locations of the restaurants serving the dish have followed where the population of Flint and, later, Genesee County, worked and shopped. As the manufacturing community in Flint has declined, many other support, dining and entertainment businesses in Flint have also closed. The future of the downtown area of Flint has become uncertain. There is concern for the future of honest, authentic Flint Coney Island restaurants within Flint and Genesee County and the simple dishes that inspired their creation. As people leave the area following the demise of automotive manufacturing in the area, expatriates in many locations are developing an interest in Simion Brayan's simple handheld creation in restaurants, coney stands and at annual events as far away as Florida, expanding the customer base for the Flint coney along the way.

FLINT CONEY SAUCE RECIPES

*R*egardless of which of the following Flint coney sauce recipes you decide to try, I encourage you to modify them as you see fit. That's part of what makes cooking, and cooking the Flint coney in particular, interesting.

HOW RESTAURANTS MAKE FLINT CONEY SAUCE

Flint Coney Spice Blend

The basic spice blend for Flint coneys is said to be equal parts chili powder, paprika and ground cumin. However, there are differences to be had for common variations of those spices, as well as the flavor of the completed sauce varying from one restaurant to the next. Here are a couple of blend sizes to start with. Adjust the ingredient types and amounts to your own taste, as the restaurants do:

For 1 pound of meat:
1 ½ tablespoons chili powder, mild or hot
1 ½ tablespoons paprika or smoked paprika
1 ½ tablespoons ground cumin
¼ teaspoon salt (optional)

For twenty-five pounds of meat:
1 ½ cups chili powder, mild or hot
1 ½ cups paprika or smoked paprika
1 ½ cups ground cumin
2 tablespoons salt (optional)

Hot or Mild Chili Powder for Flint Coney Sauce?

One of the questions to be answered when making the sauce for Flint coneys is whether to use hot or mild chili powder in the spice blend. When a chili powder container's label says only "chili powder," you can assume it's mild. Generally, only the hot chili powders are labeled as such.

But which is historically accurate? One clue we have is the published recipe for the sauce at Gillie's Coney Island in Mt. Morris, Michigan. Dave Gillie's recipe is discussed in chapter 6, with tests being described later in this appendix. In this recipe, Dave specified "chili powder (preferably hot)."

An advertisement for Gebhardt's chili powder. *From the* North Carolina Christian Advocate, *October 10, 1910.*

Chili powder is an American invention. Willie Gebhardt was born in Germany and immigrated to Texas. In wanting to use chili peppers year-round, he acquired what were likely ancho chili peppers, roasted and ground them and began offering his chili powder commercially in 1894.[225]

Gebhardt's chili powder would have been quite hot, not mild as many are today. Later commercial variations such as Gebhardt's Eagle Brand version would have been what Simion Brayan probably used in his first Flint coney shop in 1925. Gebhardt's company changed hands many times over the decades, and a current version of his chili powder is still available today.

Restaurant Preparation of the Sauce

For convenience, some chains in Genesee County may be using Abbott's 4- and 10-pound bags of raw, preseasoned and frozen Flint Coney Sauce. This would certainly save on labor costs, preparation area and so on. But those are quite recent products, which are also derived from what's described here.

Since 1925, Flint coney shops in Genesee County have always used the Koegel Coney Frank, a variation of the Koegel Vienna with less fat so it lasts longer on the grill, and the 25-pound bag of Coney Topping Mix from Abbott's Meat. This base of mostly beef heart is then prepared as follows:

I pound beef tallow, lard, shortening or vegetable oil
I ½ pounds finely chopped onion
25-pound bag Abbott's Coney Topping Mix, raw and unseasoned
I ½ cups chili powder, mild or hot
I ½ cups paprika or smoked paprika
I ½ cups ground cumin
2 tablespoons salt (optional)

Melt the fat over medium-high heat. Sauté the chopped onion until translucent. Add the Coney Topping Mix and the spices and stir well. Lower the heat and simmer 30–45 minutes, stirring occasionally.

You can also purchase the unfrozen 25-pound bag of Coney Topping Mix from Abbott's (only at the plant though, or from an Abbott's or Koegel's truck if you're a restaurant customer), divide it into 1-pound plastic bags and freeze them for later use. Once thawed, they can be prepared with the following amounts:

2 tablespoons beef tallow, lard, shortening or vegetable oil
¼ cup chopped onion
1 pound Abbott's Coney Topping Mix, raw and unseasoned
1 ½ tablespoons chili powder, mild or hot
1 ½ tablespoons paprika or smoked paprika
1 ½ tablespoons ground cumin
¼ teaspoon salt (optional)

USING YESTERDAY'S LEFTOVER CONEY FRANKS

In examining the conjecture surrounding the folklore-ridden recipe containing ground hot dogs, and in considering that some earlier restaurants may have added chopped hot dogs to be frugal and not wasteful according to their Macedonian culture, a few facts emerge:

> *The restaurants wouldn't have ground fresh Koegel Coney Franks into their sauce, but instead would have used grilled coneys leftover from the previous day. Grilling changes both the flavor and the texture, creating a more savory dish.*
>
> *As Abbott's provided Coney Topping Base to individual restaurants beginning in 1925, and as their menus were quite small, those restaurants likely wouldn't have had a meat grinder among their equipment. They may have done the chopping with a couple of bench scrapers on a cutting board or the flattop.*
>
> *The additional unseasoned meat would be cause to increase the amount of spices used in the sauce.*

I then devised a simple recipe experiment:

Grill four Koegel Coney Franks, the same number that appears in the recipe containing ground hot dogs. Refrigerate them as though for an overnight.

Follow the basic procedure for making Flint coney sauce provided earlier.

Chop the grilled coney franks to the same consistency as the Flint coney sauce.

Add the chopped coney franks to the sauce.

As the 4 coney franks are a total of about a ½ pound, add half again the amount of spice as before, along with an additional 2 tablespoons of the fat to prevent the sauce from drying out.

Simmer an additional 30 minutes.

The result ended up being quite good, as it was both familiar and something I would eat again.

PROCESSING BEEF HEARTS

Regarding grinding the beef hearts and any other meat you put through a grinder, one technique that's missing in many home kitchens is this: freeze the meat prior to grinding. If you want a finer grind, freeze it again after a first grind, then regrind it. This provides a more consistent grind and allows the intramuscular fat to be ground much more easily as well.[226] As many butcher shops offer only frozen beef hearts to begin with, thaw the heart only until you can work with it (don't thaw it completely), cut it into strips or cubes, then freeze it for the first time for grinding. Also, the finished toppings from Abbott's Meat in the 4- and 10-pound bags include onion that's ground as fine as the beef heart. To accomplish this, after cubing the beef heart to freeze it for the first time, also cube the needed amount of onion and freeze it with the beef heart. Then grind them together each time.

CHOPPING THE ONIONS FOR TOPPING

Many people chop onions by cutting the root and top off, removing the outer skins, slicing them, then roughly chopping the slices. The technique used in commercial kitchens is far simpler and faster. It also introduces a level of consistency most home cooks only see in restaurants. This is important when looking for the smaller chop seen on the coneys in older Flint coney restaurants.

Using a sweet or savory onion as a topping for Flint coneys is a personal choice, as restaurants seem divided over this. Just be sure the onions are as fresh as possible.

For the knife, an 8-inch chef's knife works best. Make sure the knife is extremely sharp, as this also reduces tearing-up when cutting onions. Sharpening with a whetstone (use water, not oil, to whet the stone) and then honing with a sharpening steel gives the best edge.

Cut the tops from the onions, leaving the roots intact.

Peel the skin off until the onions are clean and white.

Place the trimmed onions in a sealed container (not a bag) and refrigerate at 40°F for 30 minutes.

On a cutting board, from the root of the onion, cut it in half. Lay the onion on the cut side with the top away from your cutting hand.

With a target chop of about ⅛" square in mind, and without cutting into the root of the onion, make 2 or 3 horizontal cuts (depending on the size of the onion) from the bottom up that are parallel with the cutting board.

Make vertical cuts from one side of the onion to the other, again not cutting through the top, ⅛ inch in width.

The professional method here is to hold the non-cutting hand as a sort of "claw" with the tips of the fingers pulled in slightly from the knuckle, holding the onion down loosely with this claw, and moving the knife up and down against the knuckles. This prevents cutting of the fingertips. Speed can be built up with enough practice with this technique.

Finally, cut across the onion ⅛ inch in width, parallel with the trimmed top end, stopping where the other cuts end before the root of the onion. Discard the root.

Use lemon juice to clean the onion juice from your hands and the equipment you used.

Chopped onions can be refrigerated at 40°F in a sealed container (not a bag) for 7 to 10 days.

PREPARING ABBOTT'S CONEY TOPPING AND KOEGEL CONEY FRANKS AT HOME

Cooking the Topping

(Time: 45–60 minutes)

Regardless of whether you buy Abbott's Coney Island Topping (labeled as Abbott's Original Coney Island Topping in the 4-pound package) in the office area of Abbott's Meat on Blackington Avenue or order it through BuyKoegels/Lynch Shipping, it'll be frozen when you get it.

It'll also be raw: the folks at Abbott's do not cook it whatsoever.

Cooking the topping slowly to a safe temperature for serving takes time, and it's not time you really want to take when you're just cooking up some Flint coneys for a quick meal. As the topping comes in 4-pound and 10-pound tubes, Abbott's recommends cooking it off, putting smaller amounts it in quart reclosable freezer bags and freezing it. Then you can reheat only what you need when you need it, relatively quickly.

Thaw the 4-pound or 10-pound tube under refrigeration, 24 to 48 hours.

Cut the tube lengthwise and, using a large metal spoon, scrape the 4-pound bag of topping into a 6-quart steel pot. The 10-pound bag should go into two pots to cook in smaller batches.

If you have a gas range and access to a restaurant-style stainless-steel pan, known as a 4-inch hotel pan or "400 pan," you can cook an entire 10-pound tube in the pan over two gas burners.

Start the topping over medium heat, stirring regularly with a metal spoon. The topping will be like a paste.

As the topping loosens up and begins to bubble, the oils will be released from the meat. You'll need to start reducing heat to prevent scorching. Once the oil can be seen for a few minutes, reduce heat by about a third (dropping to 3.5 from 5 on a 10-point scale).

Allow the topping to continue simmering about 10 minutes, stirring regularly.

The topping will simmer and bubble harder. Depending on the thickness of the pot, reduce heat to low, 2.0 for thinner pots, 2.4 for thicker pots.

Continue to simmer 20–30 minutes, stirring regularly, until a meat thermometer measures 160°F.

> At this point, feel free to add other spices for a more personalized flavor, such as Spanish paprika, mild chili powder, cumin and so on.
> Cook for five more minutes, then remove from the heat.
> Allow to cool.

Safely cooling the topping is an important step, as organ meat is involved. A danger zone exists between 135°F (57°C) and 41°F (5°C), with the most danger of bacteria development being between 125°F (52°C) and 70°F (21°C). The bulk of this cooling needs to occur within six hours to prevent bacteria growth. The best way to do this is to spread the sauce out in glass casserole dishes, covering them with plastic wrap, and freeze them for two to three hours. They can be removed once a meat thermometer reads 41°F (5°C).

Once the topping is cool, divide it into quart reclosable freezer bags and freeze them.

To reheat, thaw the smaller amount of cooked topping under refrigeration for 24 hours. Reheat in a steel pot on the range slowly over low to medium heat until the topping reaches 160°F as read on a meat thermometer. (Note: Do not microwave, as it will change the consistency of the topping.)

Cooking the Topping in a Crockpot

If you purchase Koegel products from Koegel's on the Road, the folks who put those trips together are actually Lynch Shipping, aka BuyKoegels. com. Victoria Lynch told me she loves to put the Abbott's coney topping in the crockpot in the morning so it's ready when she's done at work for the day. That's why she includes both stovetop and her own crockpot cooking instructions in the flap of the box. But in their excitement about getting the sauce, people do tend to overlook those instructions or misplace them.

As indicated, the Abbott's sauce is shipped raw. On the package, it states it must be cooked thoroughly. Lynch told me she sets the crockpot on high in the morning and leaves it alone for 5–6 hours at that setting. She likes her coney sauce dry and crumbly, and we're certain that's likely the result. I would like to add that for real safety you should make certain to cook the sauce until a meat thermometer measures 160°F.

Finally, with either the 4-pound or 10-pound bags of topping, you'll likely want to pack and freeze the leftovers till later. Follow the steps for doing so with the stovetop instructions, and you'll be set.

Cooking the Koegel Coney Franks

There are two points to remember about the coney franks:

1. They have very little fat and were developed that way to last longer on a restaurant flattop without burning.
2. They need to be cooked low and slow to tighten the natural lamb casing to render the "snap" when bitten.

To get the snap, it's best to not cook these the way you cook any other hot dog. Even if you're used to cooking the coney frank's older sibling the Koegel Vienna over medium heat, doing so with these might burn and split them in a hurry.

> Cook the coney franks over low heat, 1.5 to 2.0 on a 10-point scale, the lower the better. Use a steel pan or skillet, or on a steel griddle. (Nonstick is all right; just don't use a bare aluminum pan, as it will get marked up over time.) Turn after five minutes, then two more times, cooking five minutes each, for a total of cooking twice on each side.

To Serve

If in Flint, get some Flint's Original Coney Buns from Mr. Bread at 2709 Davison Road (which is what Flint coney restaurants use). Otherwise, get a good utility bun like those from a foodservice supplier or a simple white hot dog bun.

> Chop a white onion, or a sweet onion if you'd like—the finer the chop, the better, all the way to a fine mince.
> Steam the buns, or microwave in pairs for 20 seconds.
> Place the coney frank in the bun.
> Spread 3–4 tablespoons of the topping on the coney frank.
> Draw 2 lines of yellow mustard the length of the sauce.
> Top with the chopped onion.

FLINT CONEY SAUCE FROM BEEF HEARTS

There's no one single recipe for Flint coney sauce, as each restaurant prepares the ground beef heart base from Abbott's its own way. This is my own version of the sauce, in a single recipe, for the stalwarts who want to try to do it all themselves.

Ingredients
½ beef heart (generally 2–3 pounds)
8–16 ounces beef kidney or ground beef (optional)
1 medium white onion
1 10-ounce package textured vegetable protein
1 cup shortening (rendered suet or tallow can also be used)
4 tablespoons Spanish or smoked Spanish paprika
2 tablespoons chili powder, mild
4 tablespoons ground cumin

Freeze the beef heart (or thaw, if it's already frozen) to about 32°F, but to no cooler than that.

Note: If adding the optional beef kidney or ground beef, freeze them the same way.

Refrigerate the onion.

Trim the harder fat from the frozen beef heart. Cut the frozen heart into 1-inch slices.

Grind the beef heart it before it thaws too much.

Note: If adding the optional beef kidney or ground beef, grind them in with the beef heart.

Put the ground beef heart into a freezer bag and distribute in the bag to an even thickness.

Refreeze the ground beef heart.

Follow the directions on the package for the textured vegetable protein to reconstitute enough to measure out one cup. Set the measured cup aside, and refrigerate any that's left for later use.

After making sure the heart is down to about 32°F again, remove the frozen ground beef heart from the freezer.

Grind the refrozen heart a second time.

Add one cup of the prepared textured vegetable protein to the meat and mix well.

Remove the onion from the fridge, mince it fine and set it aside.

In a saucepan, melt the cup of shortening over medium-high heat.

Sauté the minced onion in the melted shortening for about one minute, until the onion is translucent.

Reduce the heat to low, add the meat mixture to the saucepan and blend well.

Simmer the sauce over low heat for 30–45 minutes, until the meat is tender but also slightly juicy.

Add the paprika, chili powder and ground cumin into the meat mixture and stir well for even distribution.

Adjust the spices for personal taste as desired and simmer a bit longer before serving.

Notes

Meat grinds best when it's been refrigerated below 35°F, with the fat grinding better when it's even partly frozen. This is one step in making meat dishes that most home cooks either miss or are unaware of. In fact, commercial meat grinders are regularly located within walk-in coolers to accomplish this, with the meat not leaving the cooler until the grind is complete. And since most home refrigerators are set between 34° and 38°F (or should be set there anyway), freezing the meat to the lower temperature in the freezer instead of the fridge gives a better grind, faster.

If you want to have some sauce ready for a quick preparation at a later date, stop the procedure right after adding the reconstituted textured vegetable protein to the twice-frozen-and-ground beef heart, while it's still raw. Pack this mixture in reclosable quart freezer bags and freeze them. When you need some sauce, thaw a bag or two out, then melt your shortening, add the chopped onion, and make a batch.

Edward Abbott specifically told me in a phone call to be sure to use beef suet/tallow, not butter. David Gillie of Gillie's Coney Island in Mt. Morris, Michigan, told me in an email he uses vegetable oil, and explained they used vegetable oil at the Starlite Coney Island when he trained there.

Old-Style Flint Coney Modification

Simion Brayan is said to have based the Flint coney sauce on a Macedonian goulash made of beef heart and beef kidney.[227] Dave Gillie of Gillie's Coney

Island in Mt. Morris, Michigan, also told me in an email there was talk at the Starlite when he was there of cooks adding beef kidney to the sauce in earlier days. Beef kidneys weigh about ¾ pound each on average. If you're grinding the kidneys yourself, cut them into cubes and freeze them first. Grind them once, refreeze, then grind them again. Using the preceding recipe, add two kidneys ground as fine as the beef heart to the heart before cooking. Then continue with the recipe as described.

THE FLINT CONEY "HOLY GRAIL": THAT RECIPE FOR MACEDONIAN GOULASH

Tested November 4, 2014

It's been reported that Flint coney sauce developer Simion P. Brayan once told the following story:

> *He had eaten something at home* [in Boufi, Macedonia] *like goulash, that contained parts of a cow that most Americans would declare positively yukky* [sic]. *He concluded that to make a better coney sauce, one should blend flavorful beef heart and kidney with the beef using beef suet as a base.*[228]

Tracking down such a recipe is no mean feat. Very little record of the Macedonian dishes of the time has survived, likely because of the war in the early years of the twentieth century, and the First and Second Balkan Wars of 1912 and 1913. We do know that they would have been "nose-to-tail" eaters, as that's how people cooked back then. But even more importantly, home cooks…cooked. There were no cookbooks in those homes like there are today. Instead, like your own grandmother and great-grandmother, they simply didn't write recipes down. They learned from their own elder family members and passed them on to future generations by teaching them the dish as they cooked it.

As to the process for that goulash, we start with the following report from the same reference as the above quote from Brayan:

> *According to Edward Abbott, who eighty plus years later is still making the ground meat base for Flint's coney island sauce, the only meat ingredient is*

beef heart, regardless of the stories and rumors of other meat parts being used. Abbott's added some seasoning. . . The sauce is made by boiling commercially prepared beef suet for several hours, then browning finely chopped onions in it and adding the spices and the meat. Taste varied according to the size of the chef's hand. . . . "They still sell the traditional sauce; the meat base. . . . The Abbott product has always been sold uncooked."[229]

After quite a bit of digging, a couple of references were located that fit these descriptions, albeit without the specific meats mentioned by Brayan. The author of the blog *Delicious Tastes from Macedonia* posted an interesting recipe for Macedonian Goulash in October 2010.[230] The recipe is veal-based, but also includes a cooking process similar to that described by Edward Abbott for Flint coney sauce:

GOULASH

Ingredients
3 onions (or 4–5 if they are small)
250 milliliters sunflower oil
1 kilogram veal
Water
1 tablespoon food supplement with vegetables
Salt
1 tablespoon flour
Red pepper
Black pepper in grains

Take the peel off the onion and chop the onion. Then, squash it with hands. Next, put the onion into a big pot (take pot which is not too profound but wide). Add 200 milliliters oil. Put the pot on the oven and start cooking on low heat. Cook till the onion becomes yellow-red.

On the other hand, cut the meat on small cubes. When the onion becomes yellow-red, add the meat. Continue cooking on low heat. Also, stir from time to time. When, the meat becomes softer, add 1.5–2.0 liters of water. After that, leave mixture to start boiling (now on high heat). Add food supplement with vegetables and salt. Cook till the meat becomes soft and easy to eat. Stir from time to time.

After that, in small frying pan put 50 milliliters oil and the flour. Fry it till the flour becomes red. Then, add the red pepper. Fry 10 seconds. Next, pour the mixture into the pot. Cook 5–10 minutes. Add black pepper in grains. Finally, take the pot off the oven. Serve the goulash in the soup plates. We like it with hot pepper.

An interesting aspect of this recipe is the ingredient listed as "food supplement with vegetables." This product is called Vegeta and is made by Podravka, a company from Koprivnica, Croatia. It was originally developed by Croatian scientist Zlata Bartl in 1959. The product's basic breakdown is:

- salt max. 56%
- dehydrated vegetables 15.5% (carrot, parsnip, onions, celery, parsley leaves)
- flavour enhancers (monosodium glutamate max. 15%, disodium inosinate)
- sugar
- spices
- cornstarch
- riboflavin (for yellow coloring)[231]

There is a "clone" product called Dafinka, which is currently manufactured by Vitaminka in Prilep, Macedonia.[232] Dafinka is likely the product the preceding Macedonian recipe refers to. It's because of this 1959 product that we know this recipe isn't exactly what Simion Brayan would have remembered from earlier in the twentieth century. To fill in this obvious hole in my research, I turned to a site titled *52 Weeks in Slovakia* and its Gulas Recipe:

GULAS RECIPE

Sautee onions till golden, add 1 inch cubes of meat of equal weight to the onions—1 kilo of meat calls for 1 kilo of onions. Brown meat. Add water, wine, or beer to cover. Bring to a boil. Add 1–2 large carrots/kilo of meat grated finely. If preferred apples or potatoes can also be grated into it to thicken it instead of carrots. If pork, cook another 45 minutes. If beef, cook till tender (which may be a long time). If some other meat, cook till tender.

In the last 10 minutes of cooking add 20 grams of marjoram, 40 grams of sweet paprika, 20 grams of hot paprika, and salt to taste.[233]

This recipe fills in the holes in the former recipe but adds a couple twists in its vague descriptions; its thickening agents of carrots, potatoes or apples; and its suggestions for alcohol, which certainly don't exist in Brayan's Flint coney sauce.

Below is the recipe as I tested it, derived from Brayan's description and the two preceding recipes. A whole beef heart generally weighs about 4½ pounds. Once the fat and membranes are trimmed, the weight is about 4 pounds. This doesn't need to be exact, and really, the whole recipe is just begging for modifications. As it is, though, I hope it's quite close to what Simion P. Brayan recalled when he developed the Flint coney sauce in the first place.

OLD-FASHIONED MACEDONIAN GOULASH

Tested November 4, 2014

Ingredients
4 pounds onions
4 pounds beef heart
½ pound beef kidney (optional)
1 cup lard
Water
Salt
Black pepper
2 tablespoons smoked paprika
1 tablespoon chili powder
2 tablespoons lard
2 tablespoons flour

Chop the onions to ¼ inch.
Trim the fat and any membranes off the meats and cut into ½-inch cubes.
Melt the 1 cup of lard in an 8-quart and sauté the onions until browned.
Add the meat to the onion and lard mixture and brown.

Once the meat is browned, add enough cold water to cover the meat. Bring the water to a boil and season with salt and pepper. Boil until the meat is fork tender, 60 to 90 minutes, adding more water whenever necessary, again, to just cover the meat.

When the meat is fork tender, make a roux in a small pan from the one tablespoon each of lard and flour.

As soon as the roux form begins to form, slowly add the paprika and chili powder.

Cook for about 10 seconds, then add the spiced roux to the goulash to thicken.

Serve in bowls.

The smell of the dish can be somewhat off-putting to some, but even those diners said that the flavor and texture of this dish were quite good. To make it more palatable for Americans, serve the goulash over a bed of cooked and drained wide egg noodles and top the dish with a dollop of sour cream.

GILLIE'S CONEY ISLAND CHILI DOGS

Most online recipes and recipes in print are about as far from Abbott's original sauce as they can possibly get. They tend to be recipes that have been posted or published without being tested whatsoever or invoke the folklore-generating ground hot dog recipe from Joy Gallagher's column in the *Flint Journal* of May 23, 1978.[234]

In researching variations and specific versions of recipes for Flint-style coney sauce, I stumbled across what appears to be a diamond in the rough. This one is seriously as close to the original as I've ever seen. In researching the source, it turned out to be exactly that.

Over on her *Lost Recipes Found* website, greater Chicago–area food writer Monica Kass Rogers posted what she wrote up as the recipe for "Gillie's Coney Island Chili Dogs." Her notes on the recipe included the following statement: "Gillie's Coney Island [circa 1985 in Mt. Morris, Michigan]… shared this large-volume recipe for Flint-style Coney Island chili in a Michigan Restaurant Association cookbook more than 20 years ago."

The Michigan Restaurant Association indeed published a spiral-bound cookbook titled *A Taste of Michigan* in 1991. There are a couple things uniquely interesting about this particular recipe that illustrate its authenticity. For example, there was the process for this recipe as described by Rogers:

> *Over medium heat, melt shortening. Heat until quite hot.*
> *Add onion and sauté for 1 minute.*
> *Add spices and stir, heating for 2 minutes.*
> *Add 10 lbs of hamburger; reduce heat to very low and cook for one hour.*

This was extremely interesting because it matches the description regarding the making of the Abbott's sauce given by none other than Edward Abbott himself to an interviewer from the *Flint Journal*:

> *According to Edward Abbott, who eighty plus years later is still making the ground meat base for Flint's coney island sauce, the only meat ingredient is beef heart, regardless of the stories and rumors of other meat parts being used. Abbott's added some seasoning....The sauce is made by boiling commercially prepared beef suet for several hours, then browning finely chopped onions in it and adding the spices and the meat. Taste varied according to the size of the chef's hand.... "They still sell the traditional sauce; the meat base...that has all the seasonings—cumin, chili powder, onions and the rest of the spices....The Abbott product has always been sold uncooked."*[235]

This is the recipe as it appeared in *A Taste of Michigan*:

Gillie's Flint Coney Island Hot Dog Chili Topping

> 1. *Heat 1-1/2 cup shortening till very hot, leave on heat*
> 2. *Add 1 cup fine diced onions, cook for approximately 1 minute*
> 3. *Add 3 heaping tablespoons each of:*
>   *Paprika*
>   *Cumin (powder)*
>   *Chili Powder (preferably hot)*
> 4. *Mix spices for a couple minutes*
> 5. *Add 10# of hamburg (ground extra fine)*
> 6. *Turn heat to low, mix completely then stir occasionally for approximately 1 hour*
> 7. *Cover hot dogs (grilled preferably) in bun with generous amount of sauce, then mustard, ketchup and fine diced sweet onions as desired*

GILLIE'S CONEY ISLAND, INC.
6524 N. Dort Highway, Mt. Morris, MI 48458, 313/686-1200
In business for six years, serving American cuisine, house specialty coney hot dog; low pricing; casual attire[236]

I'll reprint Rogers's version here, with her kind permission.

Gillie's Coney Island Chili Dogs
Makes 10 lbs of chili

Flint-Style Chili Ingredients
1½ cup shortening
1 cup fine-diced onion
3 Tbsp each paprika, cumin powder, chile powder
10 lb. extra-finely ground hamburger

Hot Dog Assembly Ingredients
hot dog buns
Koegel Vienna hot dogs
mustard
ketchup (optional, frowned upon by some)
diced sweet white onion

Gillie's Coney Island Chili
Instructions

1. Over medium heat, melt shortening. Heat until quite hot.
2. Add onion and sauté, for 1 minute
3. Add spices and stir, heating for 2 minutes
4. Add 10 lbs of hamburger; reduce heat to very low and cook for one hour
5. Assemble hot dogs: Grill hot dogs (preferably a Koegel Vienna dog from Flint, MI)
6. Place dogs in buns and top with Gillie's chili, mustard, (ketchup optional) and raw diced sweet onion.

This is a lot of Gillie's coney sauce. If you eat coneys as much as we do this might be a worthwhile venture. But the amount this makes simply isn't at all family friendly. In my own version, I've adjusted these amounts to something that makes more sense for a home kitchen.

Ground beef is specified in ratios of lean meat to fat. In most foods, especially burgers, it's common to use an 80/20 ground chuck. But for this sauce I'll use more of a utility beef, a 73/27 blend, which would be more historical anyway. Since it's readily available in 3-pounds chubbs, that's the amount we'll adjust the recipe for and divide the other measurements by about a third.

Also, the spices simply specify "paprika." Most people, even some professional cooks, don't realize there are numerous kinds of paprika available. If a cook happens to have the Hungarian style in their pantry and uses it, the sauce will end up far too sweet. We'll make sure to specify the more savory Spanish paprika. A smoked paprika could also be used, with the resulting sauce being even a bit more savory.

There's also one other adjustment we want to make. This recipe calls for 1½ cups shortening. When this recipe was apparently printed, shortening had different characteristics than it does now, back in the pre–trans fat ban era of the 1980s. Still, shortening is vegetable oil, not an animal fat, and we can certainly do better in the interest of flavor.

We can replace the shortening with lard to get better richness. But remember, lard is made from pig fat. Abbott specifically mention boiling beef suet for several hours, the result of which is beef tallow. This would certainly give the sauce a more accurate flavor profile. Premium edible beef tallow is readily available in jars from FatWorks. What we can do is specify both the lard and the tallow as options, forgoing the shortening completely.

The end result of these adjustments, along with modifying the list of ingredients to match currently available products (and obviously ditching the ketchup), is below:

GILLIE'S CONEY ISLAND SAUCE (HOME VERSION)

Ingredients
3 pounds 73/27 ground beef
½ cup beef tallow (available from FatWorks) or lard
⅓ cup fine-diced white onion
1 tablespoon Spanish paprika
1 tablespoon ground cumin seed
1 tablespoon mild chili powder

Freeze the ground beef. Grind it; then refreeze and grind it again.

Over medium heat, melt the tallow or lard. Heat until very hot.

Add onion and sauté for 1 minute.

Add the spices and stir, heating for 2 minutes.

Add the hamburger; reduce heat to very low and simmer for at least one hour to let the flavors develop. Stir regularly to ensure the meat is broken up to be as small as possible.

Place grilled Koegel Coney Franks or Viennas in steamed buns and top with Gillie's chili, mustard and raw diced onion.

Notes

For the onions, just cut a couple medium onions about ⅛-inch small chop, then set aside ⅓ cup for use in the sauce.

During testing, ½ teaspoon kosher salt was added to kick up the other flavors. Doubling the amounts of the spices, especially the cumin, would certainly help. But we're not so sure paprika of any kind is a necessary part of the equation, while garlic powder or granulated garlic would certainly be a nice addition. For my own tastes, the spices should probably be 2 tablespoons ground cumin seed, 2 tablespoons mild chili powder and 1 tablespoon granulated garlic.

FLINT CONEY SAUCE RECIPE IN ABBOTT'S STYLE

Abbott's Original Coney Island Topping is available for home purchase from Lynch Shipping, in partnership with Koegel Meats, in both a 4-pound bag or a 10-pound bag at BuyKoegels.com, as well as at Abbott Meats on Blackington Avenue in Flint.

I don't have the exact recipe for this particular sauce. But I did decide to create a copycat recipe as close as possible to what's in the 4-pound bag of the complete Abbott's Original Coney Island Topping. Reverse-engineering a recipe takes a lot of work. In most instances, you have nowhere to start from. In the case of the Flint coney sauce, there are numerous clues throughout its history. Let's go through those clues one at a time …

From the "Products" page on the Koegel Meats website:

Item: Abbott's Coney Sauce…Description: This is "Flint Style" coney sauce base, manufactured by Abbott's and distributed by Koegel.…Ingredients: Beef Hearts, Beef, Water, Textured Vegetable Protein (Soy Flour, Caramel Color), Onions, Spices, Salt, Monosodium Glutamate, Sodium Nitrate, Garlic Powder, Sodium Erythorbate, Dextrose, Sugar, and Sodium Nitrite.

This current list of ingredients is rather straightforward. As to the process itself, Edward Abbott seemed quite open about it, as described earlier.

According to Edward Abbott, who eighty plus years later is still making the ground meat base for Flint's coney island sauce, the only meat ingredient is beef heart, regardless of the stories and rumors of other meat parts being used. Abbott's added some seasoning….The sauce is made by boiling commercially prepared beef suet for several hours, then browning finely chopped onions in it and adding the spices and the meat. Taste varied according to the size of the chef's hand.… "They still sell the traditional sauce; the meat base.… The Abbott product has always been sold uncooked."[237]

The last page of *Two to Go* from the Genesee Area Historical Society contains two recipes that were originally published in the *Flint Journal* by food editor Joy Gallagher on May 23, 1978. One contains ground hot dogs, which we know is not the original recipe, regardless of the rumors.

The other recipe is intriguing because of the use of beef heart as the first ingredient.

CONEY ISLAND SAUCE

1 Beef Heart
1 Lb. hamburger
2½ tsp cumin (Mexican spice)
1 t. sugar
2 small onions, chopped fine
2 t. chili powder
1 t. pepper
1 small bottle catsup
4 t. vinegar
2 tsp. salt

Simmer beef heart in water to cover until tender. Cool, then grind fine. Cook hamburger and onion in heavy skillet or saucepan until hamburger loses its red color and starts to brown. Add remaining ingredients, cover and simmer for one hour, stirring occasionally. If needed, add a small amount of water.

Of course, from the start of this recipe we know it's not the original. We know there is no hamburger, catsup or vinegar in the original, though there might be pepper. And Abbott also said the beef heart has always been uncooked. But this recipe does give us a good starting point.

THE BEEF HEART

An "average size beef heart" weighs in at approximately 4½ pounds. I'll base the copycat recipe on using a whole heart, selecting a pot to comfortably handle around 5 pounds of meat, with plenty of room for stirring.

One aspect of meatpacking and sausage making that's often overlooked is freezing the meat prior to grinding it. This ensures gristle and fat are ground as similarly as possible as the meat itself. So, if you're grinding the beef hearts yourself, cut them into cubes or strips and freeze them first. (If they are purchased frozen, thaw, then cut them into the cubes or strips and freeze.) Grind them once, refreeze, then grind them again.

The Process

Mr. Abbott mentions the first step is "boiling commercially prepared beef suet for several hours." This is called "rendering the suet," with the result being what's known as beef tallow. Some folks invariably ask, "Why not just use lard?" Lard is made by rendering pig fat; beef isn't involved whatsoever. Lard and beef tallow may be made using similar methods but have completely different flavors and are really not interchangeable.

We can either render the suet into tallow using the method described by Abbott, or we can purchase ready-made edible beef tallow. Premium edible beef tallow is readily available in jars from companies such as FatWorks.[238] What we can do is specify both routes as options.

Once we have the beef tallow, or have at least melted the suet, we need to take care of the onions. Again, Abbott says we need to be "browning finely chopped onions in it." This indicates the beef tallow should be brought to a medium heat first. The onions are almost invisible in Abbott's current product, so we'll think about going with fine to the point of almost being minced, then browned in the hot tallow.

The Other Ingredients

Let's break down the ingredient list off the Abbott's Original Coney Island Topping label. Looking at them one at a time gives us the following:

Beef Hearts—approximately 4 to 4½ pounds of ground raw beef heart, added last but listed first as it's the largest amount.

Beef—This could be the beef suet rendered into beef tallow, so that's what we'll use.

Water—This combines with the textured vegetable protein to turn the recipe into a sauce.

Textured Vegetable Protein (Soy Flour, Caramel Color)—A simple soy-based meat extender. A version from Bob's Red Mill doesn't have the caramel color, which isn't necessary anyway, and is inexpensive. In testing the recipe for Gillie's Coney Island Chili Dogs from *A Taste of Michigan* from the Michigan Restaurant Association, it became apparent the procedure requires some type of "binder" to help the loose meat become an actual sauce.[239] Textured vegetable protein (made by pressure-cooking and drying the soy flour) doesn't add additional flavor.[240]

Onions—These have been almost minced and browned in the simmering beef tallow.

Spices—This is suspected to be the cumin and chili powder Abbott mentioned, cumin being prevalent in both smell and taste in what came out of the bag containing Abbott's product. We'll use more ground cumin seed than chili powder.

Salt—Most likely this is iodized free-flowing salt, not kosher.

Monosodium Glutamate—I'm guessing this is added because the bag of sauce is a processed food. This would probably be unnecessary for a "home" version of the sauce. It's struck.

Sodium Nitrate—A preservative used in processed meats. We'll scratch this one off the list as unneeded.

Garlic Powder—We like granulated garlic better, but we'll get some good garlic powder just for this recipe.

Sodium Erythorbate—A variation of ascorbic acid, this is an antioxidant that prevents the formation of nitrosamines and has no nutritional value. Nope, we ain't using it.

Dextrose—This is generally added to commercial foods for various reasons, with a replacement ratio with sugar of 0.7 to 1 (in other words, use 0.7 cup of dextrose to replace 1 cup of sugar). Since sugar is the next item on the list, we'll just go with that, and forget the dextrose.

Sugar—Not sure why this is needed, but it's listed both on the bag and in the recipe from *Two to Go* from the *Journal*. We'll include it.

Sodium Nitrite—An additive used in processed foods to prevent botulism, we'll scratch this off the list, too.

This then gives us a list of ingredients, in descending order of measurement. I've also married this list with some of the measurements from the recipe from *Two to Go*, adding more to account for the size of the heart while not adding catsup or vinegar. I'll also have consideration for some of the measurements from testing the recipe for Gillie's Coney Island Chili Dogs. Putting it all together I finally ended up with a fully tested recipe.

FLINT CONEY SAUCE IN ABBOTT'S STYLE

Ingredients
4 pounds beef heart, approximate weight
2 pounds beef suet (to be rendered into tallow) or ½ cup rendered beef tallow
½ cup water
½ cup textured vegetable protein or soy flour
2 medium or 1 large white onion, finely chopped
4 tablespoons ground cumin seed
2 tablespoons mild chili powder
2 tablespoons iodized salt
2 tablespoons garlic powder
1 tablespoons sugar

If rendering the beef tallow from beef suet (adapted from *The Prairie Homestead*):[241]
Trim any beef off the suet and freeze for at least 24 hours.
Grind the suet.

Dump the ground beef suet into a stock pot.

Set the stock pot on a burner and set the heat to extremely low so the suet won't burn during rendering.

Wait for the suet to render.

If you wish to use pre-rendered beef tallow:

Purchase a good beef tallow, such as that which is available in jars from FatWorks.[242]

Once you have tallow available, you can begin making the sauce.

Cut the beef heart into cubes or strips and freeze. (If they are purchased frozen, thaw, then cut them into strips or cubes and freeze.)

Grind the beef heart to a fine consistency.

Refreeze the ground heart, then grind it again. Set aside.

Preheat the tallow over medium heat and add the finely chopped onions.

Allow the onions to slightly brown, just for a minute or so.

When the onions are browned, add the cumin, salt, chili powder, garlic powder and sugar and simmer for two minutes.

Remove from the heat.

Fold the ground raw beef heart and water into the seasoned beef tallow mixture and onion mixture, mixing completely.

Add the textured vegetable protein or soy flour and blend thoroughly. (As the beef heart is still raw, this is the spot where Abbott's Meats, selling the product uncooked, would bag the mixture, removing as much air as possible, and freeze it immediately. If you want to store the sauce, feel free to do the same.)

Simmer the sauce over medium heat for 30–40 minutes. Serve over grilled Koegel Viennas and top with good yellow mustard and finely chopped white onion.

OUR VERSION OF JOY GALLAGHER'S "HOMESTYLE" RECIPE

During the summers of 2008 and 2011, our family operated the Luna Pier Dog House in a beach house on the shore of Lake Erie in Luna Pier, Michigan. As far as I know, ours is the only instance of Joy Gallagher's ground hot dog recipe being used at any coney shop whatsoever. During those three months of operation in 2008, we made a total of 72 batches of the following recipe:

Ingredients
1 ¼ pounds 80/20 ground chuck
5 Koegel Viennas
1 tablespoon shortening or lard
1 tablespoon unsalted butter
1 teaspoon minced garlic
1 tablespoon prepared yellow mustard
6 ounces tomato sauce
6 ounces water
3 tablespoons mild chili powder
Kosher salt
ground pepper

Equipment
1 12" skillet
1 colander
1 meat grinder
1 8" x 8" glass dish
1 2-quart saucepan
Lid for 2-quart saucepan

Instructions
Brown the ground chuck in the skillet till it's nice and tender.

Dump the ground beef into the colander and let it drain.

Push on the browned meat in the colander with the back of a spoon until most of the grease is out, and then dump the meat into the sauce pan.

Grill the Viennas or cook them in a dry pan. Let them cool.

Install discs onto the front of the meat grinder for a fairly small grind and grind the hot dogs into the glass dish.

After digging the rest of the ground hot dogs out of the inside of the grinder, add the ground hot dogs to the browned meat.

With the exception of the chili powder and the salt and pepper, add the remaining ingredients to the sauce pan and mix it all as completely as possible.

Start heating the sauce on the stove over medium heat. When it comes to a simmer, cover the saucepan, set the burner for low heat, and let the sauce simmer for 20 minutes, stirring occasionally to prevent scorching.

Add the chili powder to the sauce and stir it in well.

Check the flavor of the sauce and add the salt and pepper to taste.

Cover the sauce again and let it simmer another 10 minutes to let the flavor develop.

Serve on grilled Koegel Viennas in natural casings on decent (not wimpy) steamed buns, all topped with a squiggle of a rich yellow prepared mustard and some chopped onion—or on nacho chips with cheese and jalapeños.

A REPRESENTATIVE FULL GREEK CONEY ISLAND MENU

oney Islands that opened in the Flint area and across the country during the latter half of the twentieth century went all-out on their menu development. Greek families added post-Tselementes dishes from their homeland, and the popularity of those dishes among non-Greeks grew as well. But the Greek owners also took the liberty of adopting dishes from other cultures, as well as regional favorites. The number of dishes on such a menu can be quite large, and the prep cooks and line cooks need to be well versed in a number of techniques.

BREAKFAST

Cinnamon Roll
Bagel with Cream Cheese
English Muffin
Oatmeal (toppings optional)
Biscuits and Gravy

Two Eggs:
As a Fried Egg Sandwich with cheese
With toast
With potatoes and toast
With ham, bacon or sausage and toast

With potatoes, toast, and ham, bacon or sausage
With potatoes, toast and corned beef hash
With potatoes, toast and 8-ounce sirloin

French Toast
Buttermilk or Blueberry Pancakes
Short Stack
Waffle with Strawberries and Whipped Cream

Breakfast Burrito—A warmed tortilla filled with seasoned scrambled eggs, sausage, red bell pepper, onion & cheese, and topped with salsa and sour cream

Skillets—Served in a sizzling skillet, topped with two made-to-order eggs, includes a side of toast
Country—Bacon, sausage, ham, potato, sausage gravy and two cheeses
Mexican—Green pepper, onion, tomato, potato, salsa, sour cream and cheddar cheese
Greek—Gyro meat, onion, potato, tomato and crumbled feta cheese

Three-Egg Omelets:
Ham and Cheese
Denver/Western/Southwestern—Ham, onions, green peppers and cheese
Mexican/Chili—Taco meat or chili, tomatoes, onions, cheddar
Mushrooms and Swiss
Steak and Onion with Swiss
Greek—Spinach, onions/scallions, feta cheese
Gyro—Gyro meat, tomatoes, shredded cucumber, sweet onion, feta cheese

STARTERS

Fried Green Pepper Rings
Fried Mushrooms
Fried Cauliflower
Fried Artichoke Hearts
Mozzarella Sticks
Jalapeno Poppers filled with cream cheese
Calamari

Potato Skins—Baked to a crisp, then covered with cheddar and bacon, broiled quickly, and topped with sour cream and chopped chives

Mixed Olive and Feta Plate with Tzatziki sauce Melitzanosalata (Spiced Eggplant) and Dolmathakia (Grape Leaves stuffed with beef and rice)—Hot or Cold, your choice

Aginares (Marinated Artichoke Hearts)

Oktapodaki (Marinated Baby Octopus)

Marinated Sardines

Saganaki (Flaming Cheese)

Saganaki Haloumi (Flaming Goat Cheese)

Kalamarakia Tiganita (Fried Baby Squid)

Yemistes (Hot Peppers stuffed with Feta)

Spanakopita (Spinach Pie)—Spinach, onion, green onion, garlic and parsley, with eggs, ricotta and feta cheese, baked in phyllo dough

Starter Combo Plat—Melitzanosalata, Dolmathakia, Aginares and your choice of Oktapodaki or Kalamarakia Tiganita

SOUPS

Chicken Noodle
Cream of Mushroom
Lentil
Split Pea
Boston Clam Chowder
Avgolemono (Chicken and Rice)
Beef Chili
Chili with Beans
Beef Stew
Lamb Stew

SALADS

Handmade Cole Slaw

Greek Salad—Seasoned greens with tomatoes, cucumber, onion, feta, Kalamata olives, capers, dressed with olive oil (grilled chicken optional)

Spanakosalata (Greek Spinach Salad)—Spinach with feta, mushrooms, onion and bacon pieces, dressed with olive oil or Greek dressing

Chef Salad—Ham, turkey, Swiss & American cheeses, tomato, egg, black olive and onion

Grilled Chicken Salad—Grilled chicken breast, egg, tomato, cucumber, onion and black olives

Turkey Salad—Oven-roasted turkey breast, bacon, cheese, tomatoes, black olives and egg

Tuna Salad—Lettuce, onion, tomato and radish, topped with a scoop of tuna sandwich salad

Cobb Salad—Greens with tomato, chicken breast, egg, avocado, onion, bacon, bleu cheese and Kalamata olives

Michigan salad—Greens with Granny Smith apple slices, chicken breast, walnuts, dried cherries, bleu cheese and a raspberry vinaigrette

CONEYS AND HOT DOGS

Flint Coney

Detroit Coney

Sauerkraut Dog

Greek Dog—Topped with tzatziki sauce, romaine, chopped black olive, feta, and red onion

Combo, two of any of the above hot dogs, with French fries and cole slaw

Loose Hamburger—Coney sauce on a soft burger bun with a slice of American cheese

Handmade Corn Dog—A grilled hot dog that is then battered and deep-fried

SANDWICHES

Also as platters, with French fries and cole slaw

Gyro Sandwich—Gyro meat, tomatoes, shredded cucumber, sweet onion, and feta cheese, topped with Tzatziki Sauce, in a Pita bread

Fish Sandwich—Perch, Trout or Whitefish

Classic Club—Turkey, ham, bacon, lettuce, tomato, American cheese and mayo on toast

Turkey Stack—Turkey, lettuce, tomato, egg, Kalamata olives and 1000 Island, served open-face

Steak and Onion—Grilled thinly shaved ribeye steak and onions, served on a toasted hoagie with banana peppers

Patty Melt—A burger patty with grilled onion and cheddar cheese on toasted rye

BBQ Pulled Pork Rueben

Classic BLT

Grilled Chicken Breast

Grilled Ham and Cheese

Artisan Grilled Cheese

Ham and Egg

Tuna Salad

Egg Salad

Wraps (variations)

Pita Sandwiches (variations)

BURGERS

All half-pound ground beef, served with French fries and cole slaw

Hamburger

Cheeseburger

Mushroom Swiss Burger

Bacon Burger

Olive Burger Deluxe—with mayo, chopped green olives and pimiento, lettuce and tomato

Gyro Burger—topped with tomatoes, shredded cucumber, sweet onion, and feta cheese and tzatziki sauce

DINNERS

Served with cole slaw or salad, two sides and choice of potato

Spaghetti and Meatballs

Macaroni and Cheese

Spanakoteropita (Spinach and Feta Pie)

Pastitsio (Baked Spinach with Cheese and Macaroni)

Moussaka (Eggplant Potato and Zucchini)
Dolmathes (Grape Leaves stuffed with Rice and Garbanzos)
Fried Shrimp
Fried Clam Strips
Fish and Chips
Fish Platter (Fried Shrimp, Clams and Whitefish)
Baked or Grilled Fish
Friday Fish Fry
Chicken Strips
Half a Chicken
Thick Grilled Pork Chops
Greek Pork Spareribs
Breaded Veal Cutlet
Veal Lemonato
Roast Beef Dinner
Liver and Onions
Steaks—16-ounce Porterhouse, 10-ounce Sirloin or Ribeye
Prime Rib—10-ounce or 14-ounce slice
Roast Leg of Lamb
Lamb Chop in Tomato Sauce

KIDS' MENU

Served with French fries and a beverage

Egg Sandwich with Bacon
Grilled Cheese
Hot Dog
Handmade Mini Corndogs
Chicken Tenders
Spaghetti and Meatballs
Fish and Chips
Flatbread Pizza
Slider Burgers
Quarter-pound Burger, cheese optional

SIDES

Fried Apples
Fried Okra
Fried Zucchini Sticks
Onion Rings and Dipping Sauces
Chicken Wings
Greek Nachos (Nacho Chips, Tzatziki Sauce, Black Olives, Feta and Jalapeño)
Greek Green Beans
Vegetable of the Day
Potatoes
French Fries, gravy optional
Loaded Fries
Poutine
Hash Browns
Garlic Mashed Potatoes
Baked or Twice-Baked Potato
Psites Patates (Greek Roasted Potatoes)

BEVERAGES

Coffee
Milk—White or Chocolate
Iced Tea
Hot Tea
Coke or Pepsi
Faygo—Crème Soda, Grape, Red Pop, Rock 'n Rye, Root Beer, Orange or
Moon Mist
Root Beer Float
Vernors Float
Vernors Cream Ale—Vernors with heavy cream
Shakes—Vanilla, Chocolate, Strawberry
Boston Cooler—Vanilla shake with Vernors

DESSERTS

Chocolate Chip Cookies with Milk
Rice Pudding
Baklava
Ice Cream Sundae
Banana Split
Brownie Sundae
Chocolate or Carrot Cake
Key Lime Pie
Custard Pie
Apple or Strawberry Pie, Ala Mode optional
Strawberry Shortcake

MICHIGAN'S "HIGHER" HOT DOG STANDARDS

*Q*ne of the most common current misconceptions is described by managing culinary director J. Kenji López-Alt over on the Serious Eats website on January 6, 2012, in "Taste Test: Natural Casing Hot Dogs from Michigan":

> *Michigan has some of the highest hot dog standards in the country, disallowing the use of mechanically separated beef, an excess of fat and offal, and limiting the amount of water a hot dog can contain to just 10%. I can't tell you for sure whether these standards actually make for better dogs since comparing a Michigan dog to a non-Michigan dog is apples to oranges, but I can tell you that the dogs sure are tasty. The best come in natural hog casings to offer snap and spring with each bite.*[243]
> [Note: López-Alt's use of the term "Michigan dog" is unrelated to that term being used for a certain chili dog served in upstate New York.]

This used to be true, but it's been quite a long time since this information was current. A law went into effect in Michigan in 1952, which, according to 1972 Michigan Department of Agriculture director B. Dale Ball, "permits only the use of inspected skeletal meat in these products. It requires a minimum of 12 percent protein....Federal law permits the use of such animal by-products as hearts, lungs, tongues, tripe, eyes, udders, lips, ears, snouts, esophagi, glands, bladders and paunches....The federal law has no minimum protein requirement."[244]

A report in the *Ludington Daily News* on October 26, 1972, stated the Michigan law had already been struck down by the Sixth U.S. Circuit Court of Appeals in Cincinnati, Ohio, in response to a lawsuit by meatpacking companies Armour, Hormel and Wilson. Ball and others from the state were planning an appeal to the U.S. Supreme Court, which refused to hear the case. This was due to Solicitor General Erwin Griswold advising the court that "Congress has explicitly excluded the states from imposing additional requirements upon meat that has been federally inspected under the federal meat inspection."[245]

The *Argus Press* subsequently reported that the Michigan delegates testified before subcommittees on June 14, 1973, in an effort to amend the Wholesome Meat Act of 1967 "and allow states to ban the byproducts and adopt any standards they choose, as long as they are at least as strict as the federal ones." Ball contended that "meat byproducts allowed under federal standards are more susceptible to contamination and can contain harmful microorganisms generally not found in skeletal beef and pork."[246]

On June 26, 1973, the *Argus Press* reported that some Michigan-based meatpackers were going to label their hot dogs as "Michigan Grade I" to show that those products were still within the spirit of the former Michigan higher standards.[247]

However, the same article reported that the USDA was amending the federal hot dog labeling laws effective that June 1. The article went on as follows:

> *1. Those made only from skeletal meat, which can contain 15 percent poultry meat, and the normal ingredients—such as water, sweeteners and curing substances—needed for processing. These products will be labeled with their traditional generic names, such as "frankfurters," "bologna" or "Knockwurst." If all the meat is from one particular species, the product will have to be labeled to show that—such as "beef frankfurter."*
>
> *2. Those made of the above ingredients plus meat byproducts—sometimes called variety meats—such as hearts, tongue, tripe, etc., and poultry meats. This type of product will have to be distinctly labeled as, for example, "frankfurters with byproducts" or "franks with variety meats." The term "with byproducts" or "with variety meats" will have to be printed so that it can be easily noticed—by being next to and in the same color and background as the generic name. The ingredient statement must specifically name each byproduct, as it is now required.*

3. Those made with either of the above formulas, plus up to 3.5 percent nonmeat binders, such as nonfat dry milk, cereal or dried whole milk, or 2 percent isolated soy protein. These products also will have to be clearly labeled—with names such as "franks with byproducts, nonfat dry milk added." And their extra ingredients will have to be named in the ingredient statement on the label.[248]

The article finished by stating that if consumers purchase Michigan products it's the consumers that will have won. Else, it's the larger meatpackers who have won.

Michigan's Food Law (the current version in 2021 having been effective since October 1, 2012) contains only the following information regarding hot dogs:

289.7119 *Other comminuted meat food products; compliance with federal regulations.*
Sec. 7119. Other comminuted meat food products, including nonspecific loaves and liver products, headcheese, blood sausage, kishka, tongue sausage, chili con carne with beans, or any other meat food products that may be allowed, shall be produced in compliance with applicable regulations of the United States department of agriculture food safety inspection service.
=====
289.7131 *Federally inspected meats; preemption of state ingredient standards. Sec. 7131. A person shall not sell or offer for sale a product that is not manufactured to the ingredient standards of this act unless the federal government legally preempts Michigan's ingredient standards. In that case, federally inspected meats not meeting the ingredient requirements of this act shall be identified as federally inspected on intact, sealed packaging from the federally inspected location.*
=====
289.7133 *Artificial casings or containers; products considered as adulterated.*
Sec. 7133. (1) All products manufactured under terms of this chapter may be sold in colored artificial casings or containers only if the products are in complete compliance with all applicable regulations of the United States department of agriculture. These products shall not be sold in colored natural casings. (2) In addition to the requirements of section 1105(1)(a), any product manufactured under the terms of this chapter is adulterated if it is the product of an animal which has died otherwise than by slaughter.[249]

It becomes apparent that Michigan's meatpackers can simply follow the federal law, with few other regulations. But it's doubtful the good ones go that route and instead follow the spirit of Michigan's former higher standards. The latter is decidedly the road to higher quality.

APPENDIX D
FURTHER READING

The Complete Book of Greek Cooking, by The Recipe Club of St. Paul's Greek Orthodox Cathedral (HarperCollins Publishers, 1990)

Coney Detroit, by Katherine Yung and Joe Grimm (Wayne State University Press, 2012)

The Detroit, Michigan, Greektown Restaurant Cookbook, by Jonathan Becklar (Solar-Vision, 2010)

Diners, Bowling Alleys and Trailer Parks: Chasing the American Dream in Postwar Culture, by Andrew Hurley (Basic Books, Perseus Books Group, 2001)

The Foods of Greece, by Aglaia Kremezi (Stewart, Tabori and Chang, 1999)

Greek Cookery, by Nikolaos Tselementes (D.C. Divry, 1956)

Home Production of Quality Meats and Sausages, by Stanley and Adam Marianski (Bookmagic, LLC, 2010)

Michigan in Four Centuries, by Dr. F. Clever Bald (Munson Michigan History Fund, 1954)

Opaa! Greek Cooking Detroit Style, by George J. Gekas (Taylor Trade Publishing, 1993)

Progressive Flint (Flint Chamber of Commerce, 1929)

Remembering Flint, Michigan: Stories from the Vehicle City, by Gary Flinn (The History Press, 2010)

Report of the International Commission to Inquire into the Causes and Conduct of the Balkan Wars (Carnegie Endowment for International Peace, 1914)

St. John St. (The "Melting Pot" Revisited), 2nd ed., by Michael W. Evanoff (Edelweiss Press, 1984)

Two to Go: A Short History of Flint's Coney Island Restaurants, by Bob Florine, Matt Davison and Sally Jaeger (Genesee County Historical Society, 2007)

NOTES

Introduction

1. Liske, "Recipe: 'Almost Flint-Style Coney Sauce', and Flint vs. Detroit Coneys."
2. Liske, "Michigan's Coney Sauces: Beef Heart? Kidneys?? The Realities Await...."
3. Liske, "Recipe: Authentic-Style Flint Coney Sauce."

1. Backstories

4. Gustin, *Flint Journal Centennial Picture History of Flint*.
5. Ibid.
6. Detroit Historical Society, *Celebrating 300 Years*.
7. Gustin, *Flint Journal Centennial Picture History of Flint*.
8. Bald, *Michigan in Four Centuries*.
9. Ellis, *History of Genessee County*.
10. Gustin, *Flint Journal Centennial Picture History of Flint*.
11. National Hot Dog and Sausage Council, "Hot Dog History."
12. Schmidt, *German Pride*.
13. Kraig, *Hot Dog*, 2009.

14. Mariani, *Dictionary of American Food and Drink*.

15. Red Hots Coney Island, "The Story."

16. Simpson and Weiner, *Oxford English Dictionary*.

17. Ibid.

18. Martyn, "Patrick Edward Abbott [234]."

19. U.S. Department of Commerce and Labor, "Manifest of SS *Main*."

20. Mackinac Center for Public Policy, "Donor Interview: John Koegel."

21. Evanoff, *St. John St.*

22. Ibid.

23. "Insurgent Garrisons Wiped Out," *Los Angeles Herald*, August 23, 1903.

24. Statue of Liberty—Ellis Island Foundation Inc. [hereafter Ellis Island Foundation], "Manifest of *SS Re d'Italia*."

25. Evanoff, *St. John St.*

26. Ibid.

27. "Insurgent Garrisons Wiped Out," *Los Angeles Herald*.

28. Carnegie Endowment for International Peace, *Report of the International Commission*.

29. Ibid.

30. Evanoff, *St. John St.*

31. Martyn, "Patrick Edward Abbott [234]."

32. Bald, *Michigan in Four Centuries*.

33. Cudahy Historical Society, "History of Cudahy."

34. Martyn, "Patrick Edward Abbott [234]."

35. Ibid.

36. Florine, Davison, and Jeager, *Two to Go*.

37. Martyn, "Patrick Edward Abbott [234]."

38. Ellis Island Foundation, "Manifest of SS *Main*."

39. Florine, Davison and Jeager, *Two to Go*.

40. Bald, *Michigan in Four Centuries*.

41. Mackinac Center for Public Policy, "Donor Interview."

42. Florine, Davison and Jeager, *Two to Go*.

43. Department of Commerce, Bureau of the Census, "Fifteenth Census."

44. Carnegie Endowment for International Peace, *Report of the International Commission*.

45. Ellis Island Foundation, "Manifest of SS *Re d'Italia*."

46. Ellis Island Foundation, "Manifest of *Olympic*."

47. Ellis Island Foundation, "Manifest of *Coronia*"; Evanoff, *St. John St.*

48. Evanoff, *St. John St.*

49. Ibid.

2. Origins of the Flint Coney

50. Red Hots Coney Island, "The Story."
51. National Archives and Records Administration, *Manifest of Passengers.*
52 Government of Canada, "Border Entry, Form 30."
53. National Archives and Records Administration, *Manifest of Passengers.*
54. Florine, Davison and Jeager, *Two to Go.*
55. Heid's of Liverpool, https://www.heidsofliverpool.com.
56. Hofmann Sausage Co., "Snappy Grillers."
57. *Flint's City Directory,* 1918–1926.
58. Ellis Island Foundation, "Manifest of the *Berengaria.*"
59. Ellis Island Foundation, "Manifest of *Olympic.*"
60. Department of Commerce, Bureau of the Census, "Fifteenth Census."
61. *Flint's City Directory,* 1918–1926.
62. Florine, Davison and Jeager, *Two to Go.*
63. Ibid.
64. Ibid.
65. Hargis, "7 British Food Habits."
66. Farmer, *Boston Cooking-School Cook Book.*
67. Rombauer, *Joy of Cooking.*
68. McLagan, *Odd Bits.*
69. Grimm and Yung, *Coney Detroit.*
70. Florine, Davison and Jeager, *Two to Go.*
71. Koegel Meats, https://www.koegelmeats.com.
72. Florine, Davison and Jeager, *Two to Go.*
73. Evanoff, *St. John St.*
74. Florine, Davison and Jeager, *Two to Go.*
75. *Flint's City Directory,* 1918–1926.
76. Florine, Davison and Jeager, *Two to Go*; Evanoff, *St. John St.*
77. Harris, "Michigans."

3. Success and Competition

78. Florine, Davison and Jeager, *Two to Go.*
79. Flint Chamber of Commerce, *Progressive Flint.*
80. Ibid.
81. Florine, Davison and Jeager, *Two to Go.*
82. Ibid.

83. Ibid.

84. Ibid.

85. Evanoff, *St. John St.*

86. Department of Commerce, Bureau of the Census, "Fifteenth Census."

87. Department of Commerce, Bureau of the Census, "Sixteenth Census."

88. Department of Commerce, Bureau of the Census, "Fifteenth Census."

89. Department of Commerce, Bureau of the Census, "Sixteenth Census."

90. Florine, Davison and Jeager, *Two to Go.*

91. Ft. Wayne Famous Coney Island, https://www.fortwaynesfamousconey
island.com.

92. Virginia Coney Island, https://www.virginiaconey.com.

93. Broder, "Daily Grind."

94. Flory, "Feeding Jackson's Astonishing Appetite."

95. Moskos, *Greek Americans.*

96. Cullari, "Citizen Lawyer."

97. Florine, Davison and Jeager, *Two to Go.*

98. Flinn, *Remembering Flint, Michigan.*

99. Karakasidou, *Fields of Wheat.*

100. Ibid.

101. Lewine, "Kaffenion Connection."

102. Flinn, *Remembering Flint, Michigan.*

103. Ibid.

104. Fellows, Annual Report of the Attorney General.

105. Aigler, "Repeals by Implication."

106. Tavern Trove, https://www.taverntrove.com.

107. Gustin, *Flint Journal Centennial Picture History of Flint.*

108. Tavern Trove, https://www.taverntrove.com.

109. Ibid.

110. Kegerreis and Hathaway, *History of Michigan Wines.*

111. Florine, Davison and Jeager, *Two to Go.*

112. Ibid.

113. Gustin, *Flint Journal Centennial Picture History of Flint.*

114. Ibid.

115. Ibid.

4. Second-Generation Coney Shops

116. Ibid.
117. Florine, Davison and Jeager, *Two to Go.*
118. Ibid.
119. Bayerl, "Life and Family of Johann and Anna Maria Bayerl."
120. Hurley, *Diners, Bowling Alleys and Trailer Parks.*
121. Lewine, "Kaffenion Connection."
122. Young, "Capitol Coney Island Offers 50-Cent Coneys."
123. Krueger, "Flint's Coney Culture Survives."
124. Wilkins and Hill, *Archestratus.*
125. Koromilas, "Feasting with Archestratus."
126. Ibid.
127. Kremezi, *Foods of Greece.*
128. Kremezi, "'Classic' Greek Cuisine."
129. Ellis Island Foundation, "Manifest for the *Thermistocles.*"
130. Tselementes, *Hodēgos mageirikēs.*
131. Ellis Island Foundation, "KLM Royal Dutch Airlines Manifest."
132. Tselementes, *Greek Cookery.*
133. Kremezi, "'Classic' Greek Cuisine."
134. Ft. Wayne Famous Coney Island, https://www. fortwaynesfamousconeyisland.com.
135. Florine, Davison and Jaeger, *Two to Go.*
136. Ibid.
137. Sanders, *Life as I Have Known It.*
138. Grimm and Yung, *Coney Detroit.*
139. Ibid.
140. Sanders, "Trip through Just-Opened Genesee Valley."
141. Hillman, "Despite Slowed Holiday Sales."
142. Florine, Davison and Jaeger, *Two to Go.*
143. Whiteside, "Burton Coney Island Opens."
144. Gustin, *Flint Journal Centennial Picture History of Flint.*
145. Adams, "Five Things to Know"; Jacobson, "Made in Michigan."
146. Florine, Davison and Jaeger, *Two to Go.*
147. Mr. Bread, "Company Story."
148. Gustin, *Flint Journal Centennial Picture History of Flint.*
149. Raymor, "Historic Flint Sign Returns."

5. Further Developments

150. *Flint's City Directory*, 1946.
151. Ibid.
152. Gallagher, "Kitchen Clinic."
153. Krueger, *Scoops*.
154. Florine, Davison and Jaeger, *Two to Go*.
155. Krueger, "Real Thing."
156. Krueger, "Coney Sauce Makes Wanted List Again."
157. Albion College, "Distinguished Alumni Awards"; Broder, "Daily Grind."
158. Khan, "Son of Koegel Meats Founder."
159. Crim Fitness Foundation, "Archived Race Results."
160. Florine, Davison and Jaeger, *Two to Go*.
161. U.S. Trademark and Patent Office, "Flint's Original Old Greek's Coney Island Recipe."
162. Michigan Department of Labor & Economic Growth, "Original Decision Report."
163. Sanders, "Trip through Just-Opened Genesee Valley."
164. Hillman, "Despite Slowed Holiday Sales."
165. Gillie's Coney Island Restaurant, http://www.gilliesconeyisland.com.
166. Krueger, "Coney Sauce Makes Wanted List Again."
167. Michigan Restaurant Association, *Taste of Michigan*.
168. *Eating Flint*, "Great Coney Conflict."
169. Crain's Detroit Business, "India Leads All Nations."
170. Grimm and Yung, *Coney Detroit*.
171. Fonger, "Flint Coney Has Passed Through Many Hands."
172. Ibid.; Grimm and Yung, *Coney Detroit*.
173. *Eating Flint*, "Great Coney Conflict."
174. Lynch Shipping Services, https://www.buykoegels.com.
175. Florine, Davison and Jaeger, *Two to Go*; Fonger, "Flint Coney Has Passed Through Many Hands."

6. The Flint Coney in the Twenty-First Century

176. Gallagher, "Kitchen Clinic."
177. Dai, "Former Bourdain Home."
178. Crawford, "Fire Closes Tom Z's Coney Island."

179. Raymor, "Historic Flint Sign Returns."
180. Krueger, "Floating Food."
181. Atkinson, "Michigan Coney Dog Project."
182. Adams, "Delphi Flint East."
183. Woodyard, "Former Ballplayer Marty Embry."
184. Refrigerated Transporter, "Evans Foodservice Acquires Meat Distributor."
185. Simpson-Mersha, "Halo Burger Is Now Offering Beer."
186. Allen, "Angelo's Famous Coney Island."
187. Acosta, "Davison Mayor Tim Bishop Dishes Out Koegel's."
188. Whiteside, "Burton Coney Island Opens."
189. Durish, "Flint Coney Owner Set to Reopen."
190. Moreno, "Scotti's Now Open 24 Hours."
191. Dresden, "Angelo's Coney Island Up for Sale."
192. Grimm and Yung, *Coney Detroit*.
193. Coyne, *Atlas*.
194. Fonger, "Gillie's Coney Island Offers Up Free Well Water."
195. Houck, "How Flint's Restaurants Are Coping."
196. Jeremy, Rutter and Park, "Events That Led to the Flint Water Crisis."
197. Corley, "Tests Say the Water Is Safe."
198. Acosta, "Flint Businesses Hurt by Water Crisis."
199. Adams, "Nearly $270K in Relief Headed to 30 Businesses."
200. Adams, "Halo Burger Chain Has New Owner."
201. Adams, "Halo Burger Food Truck."
202. Jacobson, "Made in Michigan."
203. Adams, "Five Things to Know."
204. Grow Benzie, http://www.growbenzie.org.; Michigan Department of Agriculture & Rural Development, "Michigan Cottage Foods Information."
205. Drahos, "Grow Benzie Rolls Out First."
206. Kraig, *Man Bites Dog*.
207. Ketchum, "Customers Eat around Cameramen."
208. Young, "Sig's Classic Coney Island."
209. Kalahari Resorts, https://www.kalahariresorts.com/ohio/.
210. Swig Restaurant, https://swigrestaurant.com.
211. Cape Coral Cruising Club, "Cape Coral Crusing Club."
212. Michigan State University, "Eat at State."
213. Childers, "These Are the 24 Best."
214. Dennison, "Fire Up the Grill!"
215. Ketchum, "Terry Crews Talks World's Funniest Fails."

216. Clair, "Sumptuous Delights of the Tigers'."
217. Kemp, "Detroit Coney Island Is Serving Dogs."
218. Rowe, "Should You Go to a Detroit Tigers Spring Training Game."
219. Bleier, "Feltman's, America's First Hot Dog Joint."
220. Young, "Brothers Retire after 37 Years."
221. Dortch, "Dom's Diner Opens in Former Atlas Coney Island."
222. Acosta, "Angelo's Coney Island Closes."
223. Selasky, "Red Hots Coney Island."
224. Keefer, "Retiring Gillie's Coney Island Owner Passes Business on to 17 Employees."

Appendix A

225. Arellano, *Taco USA: How Mexican Food Conquered America*.
226. Marianski and Marianski, *Home Production of Quality Meats*.
227. Florine, Davison and Jaeger, *Two to Go*.
228. Ibid.
229. Ibid.
230. *Delicious Tastes from Macedonia*, "Goulash."
231. Podravka, "Vegeta Universal."
232. Vitaminka, "Dafinka."
233. Stevo, "Gulas Recipe."
234. Gallagher, "Kitchen Clinic."
235. Florine, Davison and Jaeger, *Two to Go*.
236. Michigan Restaurant Association, *Taste of Michigan*.
237. Florine, Davison and Jaeger, *Two to Go*.
238. Fatworks, https://fatworks.com.
239. Michigan Restaurant Association, *Taste of Michigan*.
240. Bob's Red Mill Natural Foods, "TVP® (Textured Vegetable Protein)."
241. Winger, "How to Render Beef Tallow."
242. Fatworks, https://fatworks.com.

Appendix C

243. López-Alt, "Natural Casing Hot Dogs."
244. U.S. Government Printing Office, *Amend the Federal Meat Inspection Act*.
245. "Federal Court Rules," *Ludington Daily News*, October 26, 1972.

246. Johncock, "Three Times Out."

247. Ibid.

248. Ibid.

249. Michigan Department of Agriculture & Rural Development, "Michigan Modified Food Code."

BIBLIOGRAPHY

Acosta, Robert. "Angelo's Coney Island Closes after Nearly 70 Years in Flint." MLive.com. Updated December 28, 2018. https://www.mlive.com/news/flint/2018/12/angelos-coney-island-closes-after-nearly-60-years-in-flint.html.

———. "Davison Mayor Tim Bishop Dishes Out Koegel's with a Side of Politics at Specialty Hot Dog Stand." MLive.com. Updated January 20, 2019. https://www.mlive.com/news/flint/2013/05/davison_mayor_tim_bishop_dishe.html.

———. "Flint Businesses Hurt by Water Crisis to Get $25M Lifeline." MLive.com. Updated January 19, 2019. https://www.mlive.com/news/flint/2016/03/25_million_program_to_provide.html.

Adams, Dominic. "Delphi Flint East, Former AC Spark Plug Building Bought for $3.15 Million." MLive.com. Updated January 19, 2019. https://www.mlive.com/news/flint/2017/10/delphi_flint_east_former_ac_sp.html.

———. "Five Things to Know about 100-Year-Old Koegel Meats." MLive.com. February 11, 2016. https://www.mlive.com/news/flint/2016/02/five_things_to_know_about_100-.html.

———. "Halo Burger Chain Has New Owner." MLive.com. January 20, 2016. https://www.mlive.com/news/flint/2016/01/grand_blanc-based_halo_burger.html.

———. "Halo Burger Food Truck to Hit the Road Soon." MLive.com. June 10, 2016. https://www.mlive.com/news/flint/2016/06/halo_burger_food_truck_coming.html.

———. "Nearly $270K in Relief Headed to 30 Businesses Hurt by Flint Water Crisis." MLive.com. June 16, 2016. https://www.mlive.com/news/flint/2016/06/269500_awarded_to_30_businesse.html.

Aigler, Ralph W. "Repeals by Implication: Prohibition in Michigan." *Michigan Law Review* 17, no. 6 (April 1919): 495–97.

Albion College. "Distinguished Alumni Awards." https://web.albion.edu/alumni/alumni-awards/distinguished-alumni-awards.

Allen, Jeremy. "Angelo's Famous Coney Island Isn't Just a Flint Icon Anymore; Expands to Burton, Grand Blanc and Beyond." MLive.com. November 12, 2012. https://www.mlive.com/business/mid-michigan/2012/11/angelos_coney_island_opens_thi.html.

Arellano, Gustavo. *Taco USA: How Mexican Food Conquered America*. New York: Scribner. 2012

Argus Press. "Michigan's Hot Dog Law Defenders Travel to D.C." June 14, 1973.

Atkinson, Scott. "Michigan Coney Dog Project: The Face behind the Flint-Style Coney Facebook Page." MLive.com. March 28, 2012. https://www.mlive.com/entertainment/flint/2012/03/michigan_coney_project_flint-s.html.

Bald, Dr. F. Clever. *Michigan in Four Centuries*. New York: Harper & Company, 1954.

Bayerl, Andy. "The Life and Family of Johann and Anna Maria Bayerl." Bayerl Family Home Page. https://www.bo-hemian.org/documents/Johann%20and%20Anna%20Marie%20Bayerl.pdf.

Bleier, Evan. "Feltman's, America's First Hot Dog Joint, Is Making a Comeback in Brooklyn." Inside Hook. July 2, 2020. https://www.insidehook.com/article/food-and-drink/feltmans-americas-first-hot-dog-brooklyn-brothers.

Bob's Red Mill Natural Foods. "TVP® (Textured Vegetable Protein)." https://www.bobsredmill.com/tvp-textured-veg-protein.html.

Broder, Jeff. "The Daily Grind." *Metro Times*, June 27, 2007. https://www.metrotimes.com/detroit/the-daily-grind/Content?oid=2187641.

Cape Coral Cruising Club. "Cape Coral Cruising Club Facebook Page." Facebook. July 17. 2013 https://www.facebook.com/CapeCoralCruiseClub/photos/a.504518952950615.1073741829.392773167458528/504518992950611.

Carnegie Endowment for International Peace. *Report of the International Commission to Inquire into the Causes and Conduct of the Balkan Wars*. Washington, D.C.: The Endowment, 1914.

Childers, Liz. "These Are the 24 Best 24-Hour Diners in the Country." *Thrillist*, April 24, 2014. https://www.thrillist.com/eat/nation/great-american-diners-best-24-hour-diners.

Clair, Michael. "The Sumptuous Delights of the Tigers' Flint-Style Coney Dog." MLB.com. March 17, 2015. https://www.mlb.com/cut4/tigers-spring-training-flint-style-coney-dog/c-113124626.

Corley, Cheryl. "Tests Say the Water Is Safe. But Flint's Restaurants Still Struggle." NPR, March 8, 2016. https://www.npr.org/sections/thesalt/2016/03/08/469515295/tests-say-the-water-is-safe-but-flints-restaurants-still-struggle.

Coyne, Conner. *Atlas: Short Stories.* Flint, MI: Gothic Funk Press, 2015.

Crain's Detroit Business. "India Leads All Nations in Sending People to Detroit." June 1, 2014. https://www.crainsdetroit.com/article/20140601/NEWS/306019990/india-leads-all-nations-in-sending-people-to-detroit.

Crawford, Kim. "Fire Closes Tom Z's Coney Island in Flint." MLive.com. September 11, 2007. https://www.mlive.com/flintjournal/newsnow/2007/09/fire_closes_tom_zs_coney_islan.html.

Crim Fitness Foundation. "Archived Race Results." https://crim.org/races/hap-crim-festival-of-races/race-results/.

Cudahy Historical Society. "The History of Cudahy, Wisconsin." https://www.cudahyhistoricalsociety.org/cudahy-history.

Cullari, Francine. "Citizen Lawyer: Thomas C. Yeotis." *Michigan Bar Journal*, July 2011. https://www.michbar.org/file/barjournal/article/documents/pdf4article1881.pdf.

Dai, Serena. "Former Bourdain Home Les Halles Was in the Process of Being Evicted, Actually." *Eater New York*, March 30, 2016. https://ny.eater.com/2016/3/30/11327338/les-halles-eviction.

Delicious Tastes from Macedonia. "Goulash." October 19, 2010. http://delicious-macedonia.blogspot.com/2010/10/goulash.html.

Dennison, Cheryl. "Fire Up the Grill! Koegel Meats 'Always in Good Taste.'" *MyCity Mag*, June 1, 2014. http://www.mycitymag.com/fire-up-the-grill-koegel-meats-always-in-good-taste/.

Department of Commerce, Bureau of the Census. "Fifteenth Census of the United States." Flint, Michigan, 1930.

———. "Sixteenth Census of the United States." Flint, Michigan, 1940.

Detroit Historical Society. *Celebrating 300 Years of Detroit Cooking, 1701–2001.* Detroit, MI: Detroit Historical Society Guild, 2001.

Dortch, Winnie. "Dom's Diner Opens in Former Atlas Coney Island on Corunna Road." abc12.com. February 20, 2020. https://www.abc12.com/content/news/Doms-Diner-opens-in-former-Atlas-Coney-Island-on-Corunna-Road-506136551.html

Drahos, Marta Hepler. "Grow Benzie Rolls Out First Food Truck." *Traverse City Record Eagle*, May 21, 2016. https://www.record-eagle.com/news/local_news/grow-benzie-rolls-out-first-food-truck/article_1735d0af-9c00-5b60-bf78-69f21658715b.html.

Dresden, Eric. 2014. "Angelo's Coney Island Up for Sale: Ownership May Change, but Not the Taste." MLive.com. December 17, 2014. https://www.mlive.com/news/flint/2014/12/angelos_coney_island_up_for_sa.html.

Durish, Amanda. "Flint Coney Owner Set to Reopen Scotti's." *Burton View*, February 3, 2011. https://burtonview.mihomepaper.com/articles/flint-coney-owner-set-to-reopen-scottis/.

Eating Flint. "The Great Coney Conflict." September 20, 2010. http://eatingflint.blogspot.com/2010/09/great-coney-conflict.html.

Ellis, Franklin. *History of Genesee County, Michigan.* Philadelphia, PA: Everts & Abbott, 1879.

Evanoff, Michael W. *St. John St. (The "Melting Pot" Revisited).* 2nd ed. Flint, MI: Edelweiss Press, 1984.

Farmer, Fannie Merritt. *Boston Cooking-School Cook Book.* Boston: Little, Brown, and Company, 1915.

Fatworks. https://fatworks.com.

Fellows, Grant. *Annual Report of the Attorney General of the State of Michigan for the Fiscal Year Ending June 30, A.D. 1914.* Lansing: State of Michigan, 1914.

Flinn, Gary. *Remembering Flint, Michigan: Stories from the Vehicle City.* Charleston, SC: The History Press, 2010.

Flint Chamber of Commerce. *Progressive Flint.* Flint, MI: Flint Chamber of Commerce, 1929.

Flint's City Directory. Detroit, MI: R.L. Polk & Co, 1918–1926, 1946.

Florine, Bob, Matt Davison and Sally Jaeger. *Two to Go: A Short History of Flint's Coney Island Restaurants.* Flint, MI: Genesee County Historical Society, 2007.

Flory, Brad. "Feeding Jackson's Astonishing Appetite for Ground Beef Heart." MLive.com. June 4, 2014. https://www.mlive.com/opinion/jackson/2014/06/brad_flory_column_feeding_jack.html.

Fonger, Ron. "Flint Coney Has Passed through Many Hands, but It's Still One with Everything." MLive.com. December 4, 2007. https://www.mlive.com/flintjournal/onthetable/2007/12/flint_coney_has_passed_through_many_hands_but_its.html.

———. "Gillie's Coney Island Offers Up Free Well Water for Flint Residents." MLive.com. January 29, 2015. https://www.mlive.com/news/flint/2015/01/gillies_coney_island_offers_up.html.

Ft. Wayne Famous Coney Island. https://www.fortwaynesfamousconeyisland.com.

Gallagher, Joy. "Kitchen Clinic." *Flint Journal*, May 23, 1978.

Gillie's Coney Island Restaurant. http://www.gilliesconeyisland.com.

Government of Canada. "Border Entry, Form 30, 1919–1924." Government of Canada. September 9, 2020. https://www.bac-lac.gc.ca/eng/discover/mass-digitized-archives/border-entry/Pages/border-entry.aspx.

Grimm, Joe, and Katherine Yung. *Coney Detroit*. Detroit, MI: Wayne State University Press, 2012.

Grow Benzie. http://www.growbenzie.org.

Gustin, Lawrence R., ed. *The Flint Journal Centennial Picture History of Flint*. Grand Rapids, MI: William J. Eerdmanns Publishing Company, 1976.

Hargis, Toni. "7 British Food Habits Americans Will Never Understand." BBC America. July 12, 2013. https://stage.bbcamerica.com/anglophenia/2013/12/13/7-british-food-habits-americans-will-never-understand.

Harris, Sarah. "Michigans: A North Country Delicacy." NCPR News, September 3, 2012. https://www.northcountrypublicradio.org/news/story/20405/20120903/michigans-a-north-country-delicacy.

Heid's of Liverpool. https://www.heidsofliverpool.com.

Hillman, Bernie I. "Despite Slowed Holiday Sales, Business Stays Steady at Genesee Valley Center's Food Court." MLive.com. December 31, 2008. https://www.mlive.com/flinttownship/2008/12/business_keeps_up_at_court.html.

Hofmann Sausage Co. "Snappy Grillers." https://hofmannsausage.com/products/hot-dogs/snappy-grillers/.

Houck, Brenna. "How Flint's Restaurants Are Coping with the Water Crisis." *Eater Detroit*, January 21, 2016. https://detroit.eater.com/2016/1/21/10808908/flint-water-crisis-restaurant-bar-lead-filters-bottles.

Hurley, Andrew. *Diners, Bowling Alleys and Trailer Parks: Chasing the American Dream in Postwar Culture*. New York: Basic Books, 2001

Jacobson, Marc. "Made in Michigan: Koegel's Meats Celebrates 100 Years." abc.com. February 10, 2016. https://www.facebook.com/watch/?v=676512782487566.

Jeremy, C.F. Lin, Jean Rutter and Haeyoun Park. "Events That Led to the Flint Water Crisis." *New York Times*, January 21, 2016. http://www.nytimes.com/interactive/2016/01/21/us/flint-lead-water-timeline.html.

Johncock, Phyllis. "Three Times Out, Michigan Consumers Lose." *Argus Press*, June 26, 1973.

Kalahari Resorts. https://www.kalahariresorts.com/ohio/.

Karakasidou, Anastasia N. *Fields of Wheat, Hills of Blood: Passages to Nationhood in Greek Macedonia.* Chicago: University of Chicago Press, 1997.

Keefer, Winter. "Retiring Gillie's Coney Island Owner Passes Business on to 17 Employees." Mlive.com. October 21, 2021. https://www.mlive.com/news/flint/2021/10/retiring-gillies-coney-island-owner-passes-business-on-to-17-employees.html

Kegerreis, Sharron, and Lorri Hathaway. *The History of Michigan Wines: 150 Years of Winemaking along the Great Lakes.* Charleston, SC: The History Press, 2010.

Kemp, Bill. "Detroit Coney Island Is Serving Dogs at Tigertown." *The Ledger*, February 22, 2017. https://www.theledger.com/sports/20170222/detroit-coney-island-is-serving-dogs-at-tigertown.

Ketchum, William E. "Customers Eat around Cameramen as TLC Films Reality Pilot at Starlite Diner." MLive.com. November 2, 2012. http://www.mlive.com/entertainment/flint/index.ssf/2012/11/tlc_films_pilot_at_starlite_di.html.

———. "Terry Crews Talks 'World's Funniest Fails,' #OscarSoWhite Controversy, and Why College Athletes Should Be Paid." MLive.com. January 16, 2015. http://www.mlive.com/entertainment/flint/index.ssf/2015/01/terry_crews_talks_worlds_funni.html.

Khan, Bill. "Son of Koegel Meats Founder Will Run His Third Crim 10-Mile Race at Age of 84." MLive.com. August 25, 2010. http://blog.mlive.com/flintjournal/runners/2010/08/082510-crim.html.

Koegel Meats. https://www.koegelmeats.com.

Koromilas, Kathryn. "Feasting with Archestratus." *Odyssey, The World of Greece*, November/December 2007.

Kraig, Bruce. *Hot Dog: A Global History.* London, UK: Reaktion Books–Edible, 2009.

———. *Man Bites Dog: Hot Dog Culture in America.* Lanham, MD: AltaMira Press, 2014.

Kremezi, Aglaia. "'Classic' Greek Cuisine: Not So Classic." *The Atlantic*, July 2010. https://www.theatlantic.com/health/archive/2010/07/classic-greek-cuisine-not-so-classic/59600/.

———. *The Foods of Greece*. New York: Stewart, Tabori and Chang, 1999.

Krueger, Ron. "Coney Sauce Makes Wanted List Again." *Flint Journal*, January 6, 1998.

———. "Flint's Coney Culture Survives at Starlite Diner." MLive.com. December 9, 2010. http://www.mlive.com/dining/flint/index.ssf/2010/12/flints_coney_culture_survives_at_starlite_diner.html.

———. "Floating Food: Couples Serve Up Concessions from Pontoon Boat on Argentine Township Lake." MLive.com. July 14, 2008. http://www.mlive.com/entertainment/flint/index.ssf/2008/07/floating_food_couples_serve_up.html.

———. "The Real Thing." *Flint Journal*, April 18, 1995.

———. *Scoops*. Flint, MI: Flint Journal, 2000.

Lewine, Edward. "The Kaffenion Connection: How the Greek Diner Evolved." *New York Times*, April 14, 1996.

Liske, Dave. "Recipe: 'Almost Flint-Style Coney Sauce', and Flint vs. Detroit Coneys." Mlive.com. October 15, 2007. https://www.mlive.com/michigan_appetite/2007/10/recipe_almost_flintstyle_coney.html

———. "Michigan's Coney Sauces: Beef Heart? Kidneys?? The Realities Await." Luna Pier Cook, January 28, 2009. http://micuisine.com/lunapiercook/?p=1324

———. "Recipe: Authentic-Style Flint Coney Sauce." Luna Pier Cook, September 27, 2009. http://micuisine.com/lunapiercook/?p=2055

Los Angeles Herald. "Insurgent Garrisons Wiped Out—Three Villages near Fiorina Have Been Abandoned." August 23, 1903.

López-Alt, J. Kenji. "Natural Casing Hot Dogs From Michigan | Taste Test." *Serious Eats*. August 10, 2018. https://www.seriouseats.com/taste-test-natural-casing-hot-dogs-from-michigan.

Ludington Daily News. "Federal Court Rules Michigan Hot Dogs Are Too High a Standard." October 26, 1972.

Lynch Shipping Services. https://www.buykoegels.com.

Mackinac Center for Public Policy. "Donor Interview: John Koegel." May 2, 2013. https://www.mackinac.org/18589.

Mariani, John F. *The Dictionary of American Food and Drink*. Boston, Massachusetts: Ticknor & Fields, 1983.

Marianski, Stanley, and Adam Marianski. *Home Production of Quality Meats and Sausages*. Seminole, FL: Bookmagic, 2010.

Martyn, Scott H. "Patrick Edward Abbott [234]." *Martyn Family History.* http://familyhistory.themartyns.net/familyfiles/234.htm.

McLagan, Jennifer. *Odd Bits: How to Cook the Rest of the Animal.* Berkeley, CA: Ten Speed Press, 2011.

Michigan Department of Agriculture & Rural Development. "Michigan Cottage Foods Information." https://www.michigan.gov/mda rd/0,4610,7-125-50772_45851-240577--,00.html.

———. "Michigan Modified Food Code, As Adopted by the Michigan Food Law Effective October 1, 2012." October 1, 2012. https://www.michigan.gov/documents/mdard/MI_Modified_2009_Food_Code_396675_7.pdf.

Michigan Department of Labor & Economic Growth. "Original Decision Report from 07-01-2006 to 07-31-2006." July 31, 2006. https://www.michigan.gov/documents/julydet_167514_7.pdf.

Michigan Restaurant Association. *A Taste of Michigan.* Lansing: Michigan Restaurant Association, 1991.

Michigan State University. "Eat at State." https://eatatstate.msu.edu.

Moreno, Tara. "Scotti's Now Open 24 Hours." *Burton View*, February 13, 2014. https://burtonview.mihomepaper.com/articles/scottis-now-open-24-hours/.

Moskos, Charles C. *Greek Americans: Struggle and Success.* New Brunswick, NJ: Transaction Publishers, 1989.

Mr. Bread. "Company Story." http://mrbread.net/history.asp.

National Archives and Records Administration. Manifest of Passengers Arriving in the St. Albans, VT District through Canadian Pacific, and Atlantic Ports, 1895–1954. Washington, D.C.: National Archives and Records Administration, 1921.

National Hot Dog and Sausage Council. "Hot Dog History." http://www.hot-dog.org/culture/hot-dog-history.

Podravka. "Vegeta Universal." https://www.podravka.com/product/vegeta-universal/.

Raymor, Marjory. "Historic Flint Sign Returns with New Flint Original Coney Island Restaurant." MLive.com. May 31, 2008. https://www.mlive.com/flintjournal/business/2008/05/historic_flint_sign_returns_wi.html.

Red Hots Coney Island. "The Story…" http://redhotsconeyisland.com/history.html.

Refrigerated Transporter. "Evans Foodservice Acquires Meat Distributor." June 1, 2005. http://refrigeratedtransporter.com/archive/evans-foodservice-acquires-meat-distributor-0.

Rombauer, Irma S. *Joy of Cooking.* New York: Charles Scribner's Sons, 1957.

Rowe, Kellie. "Should You Go to a Detroit Tigers Spring Training Game in Lakeland, Florida?" *Fox 2 Detroit.* March 7, 2019. https://www.fox2detroit.com/news/should-you-go-to-a-detroit-tigers-spring-training-game-in-lakeland-florida.

Sabella, Anthony. "Koegel Meats Donates $35,000 to Band Program at Flint Community Schools." abc12.com. December 16, 2015.

Sanders, Col. Harlan. *Life as I Have Known It Has Been Finger Lickin' Good.* Carol Stream, IL: Creation House, 1974.

Sanders, Rhonda. "Trip through Just-Opened Genesee Valley Reveals a Brand-New World of Shopping." *Flint Journal*, August 8, 1970.

Schmidt, Gretchen. *German Pride: 101 Reasons to Be Proud You're German.* Toronto, CAN: Citadel Press, 2003.

Selasky, Sue. "Red Hots Coney Island in Highland Park to Close Doors after 100 Years in Business." *Detroit Free Press*, June 19, 2021. https://www.freep.com/story/entertainment/dining/2021/06/19/red-hots-coney-island-highland-park/7739058002/.

Simpson, John, and Edmund Weiner. *Oxford English Dictionary.* Oxford, UK: Clarendon Press, 1989.

Simpson-Mersha, Isis. "Halo Burger Is Now Offering Beer at One of Its Restaurants." MLive.com. August 26, 2019. https://www.mlive.com/news/saginaw-bay-city/2019/08/halo-burger-is-now-offering-beer-at-one-of-its-restaurants.html.

The Statue of Liberty—Ellis Island Foundation Inc. "KLM Royal Dutch Airlines Manifest, Flight KL 631, Aircraft No. PH-TDK." https://heritage.statueofliberty.org/passenger-details/czoxMzoiOTAxMTg2Njc3MTgxMiI7/czo4OiJtYW5pZmVzdCI7.

———. "Manifest for the *Thermistocles*, December 15, 1920." https://heritage.statueofliberty.org/passenger-details/czoxMjoiMTAwMzIzMTEwMzgwIjs=/czo4OiJtYW5pZmVzdCI7.

———. "Manifest of *Caronia*." https://heritage.statueofliberty.org/passenger-details/czoxMjoiMTAwODEzMDYwMjU4Ijs=/czo4OiJtYW5pZmVzdCI7.

———. "Manifest of *Olympic*." https://heritage.statueofliberty.org/passenger-details/czoxMjoiOTAxNzAzMjAyMjE4Ijs=/czo4OiJtYW5pZmVzdCI7.

———. "Manifest of SS *Re d'Italia*." https://heritage.statueofliberty.org/passenger-details/czoxMjoiNjEwMTcwMDEwMDglIjs=/czo4OiJtYW5pZmVzdCI7.

———. "Manifest of SS *Main*." https://heritage.statueofliberty. org/passenger-details/czoxMjoiMTAxMTkzMTgwMjM3Ijs=/ czo4OiJtYW5pZmVzdCI7.

———. "Manifest of the *Berengaria*." https://heritage.statueofliberty. org/passenger-details/czoxMjoiOTAxNzU5OTQyMTUyIjs=/ czo4OiJtYW5pZmVzdCI7.

Stevo, Allan. "Gulas Recipe." *52 Weeks in Slovakia*. http://www.52insk.com/ footnotes-to-slovak-culture/gulas-recipe/.

Swig Restaurant. https://swigrestaurant.com.

Tavern Trove. https://www.taverntrove.com.

Tselementes, Nicholas. *Greek Cookery*. New York: D.C. Divry, 1956.

———. *Hodēgos mageirikēs*. Greece: Ekdosis V. Papachrysanthou, 1930.

U.S. Government Printing Office. *Amend the Federal Meat Inspection Act: Hearings, Ninety-Third Congress, First Session*. Washington, D.C.: U.S. Government Printing Office, 1973.

U.S. Trademark and Patent Office. "Flint's Original Old Greek's Coney Island Recipe—Trademark Details." Justia Trademarks. June 22, 1990. https://trademarks.justia.com/733/07/flint-s-original-old-greek-s- coney-island-recipe-73307706.html.

Virginia Coney Island. https://www.virginiaconey.com.

Vitaminka. "Dafinka." https://vitaminka.com.mk/en/products/dafinka-4.

Whiteside, Mary Ann Chick. "Burton Coney Island Opens Under New Ownership." MLive.com. February 2, 2008. https://www.mlive.com/ flintjournal/onthetable/2008/02/burton_coney_island_opens_under_ new_ownership.html.

Wilkins, John, and Shaun Hill. *Archestratus: Fragments from the Life of Luxury*. London, UK: Prospect Books, 2011.

Winger, Jill. "How to Render Beef Tallow (Updated)." The Prairie Homestead. June 5, 2012. https://www.theprairiehomestead. com/2012/02/how-to-render-beef-tallow.html.

Woodyard, Eric. "Former Ballplayer Marty Embry's Southern-Themed '51 to Go' Restaurant Cooks Slam-Dunk Meals in Flint." MLive.com. June 13, 2014. https://www.mlive.com/entertainment/flint/2014/06/ former_ballplayer_marty_embrys.html.

Young, Gordon. "Sig's Classic Coney Island." *Flint Expatriates*. May 6, 2008. http://www.flintexpats.com/2008/05/sigs-classic-coney-island.html.

Young, Molly. "Brothers Retire after 37 Years of Food and Friends at Atlas Coney Island." MLive.com. March 22, 2017. http://www.mlive.com/ news/flint/index.ssf/2017/03/brothers_80_and_82_announce_re.html.

———. "Capitol Coney Island Offers 50-Cent Coneys for Restaurant's Anniversary." MLive.com. June 19, 2016. https://www.mlive.com/news/flint/2016/07/capitol_coney_island_offers_50.html.

ABOUT THE AUTHOR

A graduate of Grand Blanc High School, Dave Liske has been a technical writer for the U.S. Navy, the Toyota Technical Center and the University of Michigan, as well as having written and tech-reviewed computer programming books for Wrox Press in the United Kingdom. A former kitchen manager, he began writing the *Luna Pier Cook* food blog for the *Monroe News* in 2006 and operated a popular Flint Coney stand at the Lake Erie Beach in Luna Pier, Michigan, during the summer of 2008 with his stepson Caleb and the other five kids he and his wife, Mary, share. With Mary now working as a travel nurse, Dave is making Flint coneys both for home meals and for Mary's coworkers to enjoy on occasion, from Wyoming to Maine. Dave maintains the *Flint Coney Resource Site*, a companion blog for this book including other related recipes and a current list of restaurants serving the Flint coney, at http://flintconeys.com.

Visit us at
www.historypress.com